Spiritual Classics
Series

World Wisdom

The Library of Perennial Philosophy

The Library of Perennial Philosophy is dedicated to the exposition of the timeless Truth underlying the diverse religions. This Truth, often referred to as the *Sophia Perennis*—or Perennial Wisdom—finds its expression in the revealed Scriptures as well as the writings of the great sages and the artistic creations of the traditional worlds.

Naturalness: A Classic of Shin Buddhism appears as one of our selections in the Spiritual Classics series.

Spiritual Classics Series

This series includes seminal, but often neglected, works of unique spiritual insight from leading religious authors of both the East and West. Ranging from books composed in ancient India to forgotten jewels of our time, these important classics feature new introductions which place them in the perennialist context.

Cover calligraphy by Shinran, the 13th century
founder of Shin Buddhism.
Namu-amida-butsu: "Adoration to the Buddha
of Infinite Light." In Shin Buddhism this Name of Amida
Buddha is the traditional *prayer of the heart.*

Naturalness

A Classic of Shin Buddhism

by

Kenryo Kanamatsu

Introduction by
Reverend Tetsuo Unno

World Wisdom

Naturalness:
A Classic of Shin Buddhism
by Kenryo Kanamatsu

©2002 World Wisdom, Inc.

Most Recent Printing Indiciated by last digit below:

10 9 8 7 6 5 4 3 2

ISBN 13 for second prining:
978-0941532-29-7

Library of Congress Cataloging-in-Publication Data

Kanamatsu, Kenryo, 1915-1986.
    Naturalness: A Classic of Shin Buddhism / by Kenryo Kanamatsu ; introduc-
tion by the Reverend Tetsuo Unno.
        p. cm. — (Spiritual classics)
    ISBN 0-941532-29-1 (pbk. : alk. paper)
    ISBN 0-941532-34-8 (cloth : alk. paper)
    1. Shin (Sect)—Doctrines. 2. Pure Land Buddhism—Doctrines. I. Title.
II. Spiritual classics (Bloomington, Ind.)
BQ8718.3 .K343 2002
294.3'926—dc21

                                                                    2001006298

Printed on acid-free paper in United States of America

For information address World Wisdom, Inc.
P.O. Box 2682, Bloomington, Indiana 47402-2682

www.worldwisdom.com

Contents

Publisher's Foreword

Pure Land is the flower of Japanese Buddhism. Although it is less well known in the West than Zen, Vipassana, or Tibetan Buddhism, its message of holy freedom, or naturalness, which arises when man conforms with sincere attachment to the eternal saving will of the Buddha, has been an illuminating way of spiritual awakening for multitudes of Japanese people since the sixth century when Buddhism came to Japan.

Kanamatsu's *Naturalness*, written in 1949, is more than an introduction to the essence of Shin Buddhism, the final development of Pure Land Buddhism. It is a profound and enlightened meditation on the relationship between man and Amida Buddha, who is pure mercy and whose Name is a vehicle of Nirvanic Reality. Combining the erudition of a philosopher with the sensitivity of a poet, Kanamatsu leads the reader into the heart of the subject where man may unite with the

Buddha-Nature even in the ordinary activities of everyday life. The deep compassion and beautiful simplicity of this classic work—which like a haiku speaks volumes with few words—will appeal to all people who seek a spiritual antidote to the artificiality and ugliness that causes much of the suffering in our world.

Very few books have appeared in the West on the Shin tradition, yet D.T. Suzuki—recognized as the foremost exponent of Buddhism to western culture—has characterized Shin Buddhism as Japan's major religious contribution to the West. Kanamatsu's *Naturalness* allows the reader to experience that "even here lies the other shore waiting to be reached—yes, here is the Eternal Present, not distant, not anywhere else."

World Wisdom
Bloomington, Indiana
January, 2002

Introduction

In the West, Buddhism, for the most part, means Zen Buddhism, Tibetan, or Vipassana Buddhism. And, it does not bear repeating that all three share a profundity and depth that is Absolute and comprise authentic Paths toward Enlightenment.

Their final goal, the perfect annihilation of one's ego and its outward manifestation in the form of an unprejudiced and egoless Compassion toward all beings, however, may be, for most, impossible to attain or practice. In short, their Paths may be beyond the capacity of most to bring to final fruition; that is, to truly actualize or to realize.

For them, the Shin Buddhism of Shinran offers an alternative Path. In his work, *Naturalness*, the author, with tremendous urgency and bodhisattvic compassion, attempts to convey, especially to western readers, Shin Buddhism's heart and its essence.

He does so, to paraphrase V. Nabakov's description of the ideal reader, not merely with his brain, or his heart, but with his brain, heart, and his spine. That is, with the totality of his being, and most crucially with his Faith, the attendant liberation, and eventual Enlightenment. The latter three having their genesis in a Power other than his own; that is, in the "Other Power" (*Tariki*), the salvific Power of the Amida Buddha.

The author's sense of urgency and his passion, as might be expected, shapes the tenor and character of his book. For example, in the attempt to be truly understood, that is, understood in an existential manner, he unhesitatingly employs new words and terminologies. In place of "*Prajna*," he uses "pure feeling"; for "Compassion," "Love"; for Amida Buddha, "Unthinkable Timeless Being," among others.

The author has chosen to approach his work in a manner that might be described as being, in essence, experiential or existential, intuitive and poetic, as opposed to that which might be characterized as being intellectual or conceptual, systematic, or prosaic.

With regard to his description of Shin Buddhism, it must first be noted that at their deepest point, all religions transcend reason; in short, ultimately religions are paradoxical. For example, those phenomena that stand in logical opposition to each other are declared to be One; that is, in a state of "coincidence of opposites." The author takes great pains throughout his work to note the presence of such coincidences, a sign of great religious depth, in Shin Buddhism.

In brief, he refers to (and here, we follow the author's phrasing) man's "abysmal sinfulness" and its Oneness with the "Unthinkable Power" that saves that abysmally sinful man. He writes of the Oneness of the "I" and the "Thou." Of the finite "I am" and the Eternal "I Am." Of our utterance of the *Nembutsu* and Amida's utterance of the *Nembutsu.* Of our longing to become Eternal and Amida's longing for us to become so. Of our love and His Everlasting Love. Of the indwelling light and Amida's Light. Of absolutely dying unto the self and the absolute rebirth of the self in the Universal Self. Of forms and the Formless. Of passivity and Activity. Of this world and the spiritual world, i.e. the Pure Land. Metaphorically, of man and his Parent; of the stream and the Ocean.

He writes of "pure feeling" or *Prajna* as being a knowledge that knows and knows not; as being an intuition that does not intuit or as a thought that is not a thought. Or, that suffering harbors within itself the infinite possibility of perfection and the unfolding of joy Eternal.

The author, moreover, emphasizes that such paradoxical coincidences cannot be apprehended or resolved by the exercise of reason; that they can only be fully apprehended and resolved by "pure feeling," i.e.

by intuitive insight. That is to say, one attains the Truth, not by gradual ascension as in the case of Jacob's ladder, but abruptly, in a transcendent leap. In Shin Buddhist terminology, "a transcendent leap to the side," as opposed to a seeming progress forward which is, in reality, without end and therefore, is ultimately futile. (In Japanese, *Ocho.*)

He further makes the crucial point that the Power that enables man to make that infinite leap has its origins in a Power absolutely other than his own; that is, in the Other Power, *Tariki,* of Amida Buddha.

In the last section, the author describes how being One with an opposite results in freedom. That is, if one regards karma as being a phenomenon that stands outside of, or external to oneself, there comes into being that which binds and that which is bound. But when one is identified and fused with one's karma, while continuing to exist in karma, one is no longer of karma. That is, one is free of karma's harmful effect, since both the active agent that harms and the passive agent that is harmed are both obliterated in the emerging Oneness.

Although a work of great subjectivity, a work of profound personal and religious commitment, the author takes great pains to provide an objective framework for that subjectivity. Therefore, throughout his work, references are made to basic Shin Buddhist texts: the *Larger Sukhavativyuha*, the *Amitayur-dhyana*, and the *Smaller Sukhavativyuha Sutras*, Shinran's *Kyo-gyo-shin-sho*, Zendo's *Sanzengi*, Yuien's *Tannisho*, the writing of the Tokugawa Priest Gido, the collateral text *Anjin-ketsujosho*, and finally, to a living example of Shin Buddhist Faith in the person of the unlettered and yet indescribably deep Shoma, the Myokonin.

This work, *Naturalness*, was first published nearly fifty years ago. With this republication, and Buddhist Churches of America's reissue several years ago, it is, I firmly believe, the author's devout wish, fueled by his awareness of Shin Buddhism's absolute depths, that a new generation of readers gain access to it and through it, the teaching of Shin Buddhism.

Should this come to pass, to whatever degree, the author will feel, I believe, more than amply recompensed for his effort, and the depth of his rejoicing can only be imagined.

Rev. Tetsuo Unno
August 26, 2001
Los Angeles, California

Author's Preface

Japanese Buddhism may be regarded in many ways as the most representative form of Buddhism, and Shin Buddhism, or *Shinshu* as it is called in Japan, in which we see the deep meaning of deliverance by faith most thoroughly revealed, is the efflorescence of Japanese Buddhism. This book is a humble attempt to introduce the essence of Shin Buddhism to the western reader.

The subject-matter of this book has not been treated in the Buddhologist's way of approach. All the great utterances of man have to be judged not by the letter but by the spirit. The meaning of the living words that come out of the inmost experiences of great hearts can never be exhausted by any one system of logical interpretation. To me, the words of Buddhist *Sutras* (Scriptures) and the teaching of Shinran (1173-1263), the founder of Shin Buddhism (*Shin-shu*), have ever been things of the spirit, and therefore instinct with individual meaning for me, as for others, and awaiting for their conformation my own individual testimony.

The writer has been brought up in a Buddhist temple where texts of *Shinshu* are used in daily worship, and he feels deep affection for Shinran, who explained the meaning of the living words of Shakyamuni, the founder of Buddhism, by the commentary of his own individual life, living the life of a holy freedom or *naturalness* in the closest communion with Amida (*Amitabha*), the Great Compassionate One. So, in this book, it may be hoped, the western reader will have an opportunity of coming into touch with the *true* spirit of Buddhism as revealed in the sacred texts of *Shinshu* or the True (*Shin*) Religion (*shu*) and manifested in the actual life of its devout followers.

I should acknowledge that in the writing of this book I am greatly indebted to Dr. Daisetsu T. Suzuki's *The Essence of Buddhism* (1948) and the late Rev. Gessho

Sasaki's *A Study of Shin Buddhism* (1925), among other books. How much I have been helped, as regards wording and illustration, by Rabindranath Tagore's *Sadhana* will be evident to all who know that great work.

I should add that in translating from the *Dai-muryoju-kyo*, the *Kyo-gyo-shin-sho*, and the *Tanni-sho*, I have got great help from *The Shinshu Seiten* (*The Holy Scripture of Shin-shu*) published lately by the Honpa Hongwanji Mission of Hawaii.

In conclusion, I wish to express my hearty gratitude to my friend Rev. Bumpo Kuwatsuki of Los Angeles for enabling the publication of this revised and enlarged edition of my first book, *Amitabha—The Life of Naturalness* (1949), which has been long out of print.

Kenryo Kanamatsu
Kyoto, Japan
8 IV 1955

Naturalness

A Classic of Shin Buddhism

I

Pure Feeling

1

Buddhism is a religion of "Enlightenment" (*satori*) as is shown by the term *Buddha,* which means the *Enlightened One.* When man attains *Bodhi,* i.e. the awakenment from the self-obscured ignorance to the perfection of consciousness, he becomes a Buddha. In other words, *Bodhi* or Enlightenment is the freedom from the ignorance that darkens our consciousness by limiting it within the boundaries of our personal self, and obstructs our vision of truth. Truth is all-comprehensive. There is no such thing as absolute isolation in existence, and the only way of attaining truth is

---

through the interpenetrating of our being into all objects. It is dire destruction for us when we envelop our consciousness in a dead shell of our narrow self. This is indeed the killing of the very spirit of our being, which is the spirit of comprehension and permeation. Essentially man is not a slave of himself, or of the world, but he is a *lover.* Our freedom and fulfillment is in perfect comprehension and permeation. By this power of comprehension, this permeation of our being, our hearts are *transferred back* into, and united with the All-pervasive Original Heart, which is the Heart of our hearts.

However, being shut up within the narrow walls of our limited self, we lose our *simplicity* and turn a deaf ear to the *call* welling up from the inmost depths of our heart. We are not quite conscious of our *inherent longing,* for it is hidden under so many layers of pride and self-deception. Just as we are not ordinarily conscious of the air, so we are apt to overlook the claims of the *heart* demanding our foremost attention. But when we meet happenings incompatible with our selfish desires and baffling human calculations, we are made to pause and reflect on the feebleness of our earthly desires. This is the time when the *heart* asserts itself and forces us to look beyond our narrow self. Here we feel an *unthinkable power* stronger than ourselves, compelling us to choose between the self and the not-self, between ignorance and enlightenment. This Unthinkable Power stronger than ourselves, this persistent *urge* impelling the self to transcend itself, is a *call* to us of the All-feeling Compassionate Heart, the Eternal Spirit of Sympathy—who is in his essence the Light and Life of all who is World-conscious. To feel all, to be conscious of everything, is the Spirit. We are immersed in his consciousness body and soul. It is through his consciousness that the sun attracts the earth; it is through his consciousness that the light waves are being transmitted from planet to planet. Not only in space, but this Light and Life, this All-feeling Being is in our hearts.

He is all-conscious in space, or the world of extension; and he is all-conscious in heart, or the world of intention. He is working in the inmost recesses of our heart as the *innate love*—that *basal, pure, universal-feeling* that interpenetrates all objects, that moves and exists in unbroken continuity with the outer world. Our self has ceaselessly to shed its limits in oblivion and death, and repeatedly sink into this basal *pure feeling*. It must dive boldly into the depths of existence, touch the Fundamental Unity, and follow the eternal rhythm of the World's Heart so as to become *one* with the all.

The enlightened man, with his inner perspective deepened and enlarged, meets the One Eternal Spirit in all objects. He realizes the wholeness of his existence by disclosing the One Living Truth everywhere that makes all realities true. In his mind's eye, it reflects something supernatural. The water does not merely cleanse his limbs, but it purifies his heart, for it touches his spirit. The earth does not merely hold his body, but it gladdens his mind, for its contact is more than a physical contact—it is a living presence of the Glory of Amida[1]—the Eternal Spirit. This is not mere knowledge, as science is, but it is an intuition of the spirit by the spirit. This is where Buddha speaks to Buddha. Amida's revelation is not to be sought after by our own efforts; it comes upon us by itself, of its own accord. Amida is always in us and with us, but by means of our human understanding we posit him outside us, against us, as opposing us, and exercise our intellectual power to the utmost to take hold of him. The revela-

[1] Amida (Amita) in Japanese Buddhism stands for both *Amitabha*, Infinite (*amita*) Light (*abha*) and *Amitayus*, Eternal (*amita*) Life (*ayus*). See Chapter III and IV.

tion, however, would take place only when this human power has been really exhausted, has given up all its selfishness, when we have come back to our *simplicity.* We can only *feel* him as Heart of our heart and Spirit of our spirit; we can only *feel* him in the love and joy we feel when we give up our self and stand before him face to face.

2

The spirit of renunciation is the deepest reality of the human heart. Our self can realize itself truly only by giving itself away. In *giving* (*dana*) is our truest joy and liberation, for it is uniting ourselves to that extent with the Infinite. We grow by losing ourselves, by uniting. Gaining a thing is by its nature partial, it is limited only to a particular want, but giving is complete, it belongs to our wholeness, it springs not from any necessity but from our affinity with the Infinite, which is the principle of unity and perfection that we have in our inmost heart. Our abiding happiness is not in getting anything, but in giving ourselves up to what is greater than ourselves, to the infinite ideal of perfection.

All our belongings assume a weight by the ceaseless gravitation of our selfish desires; we cannot easily cast them away from us. They seem to belong to our very nature, to stick to us as a second skin, and we bleed as we detach them. "It is easier for a camel to pass through the eye of a needle than for a rich man to enter the kingdom of heaven." He who is bent upon accumulating riches is unable, with his ego continually bulging, to pass through the gate of the *spiritual world* which is the world of perfect harmony with the all; he is shut up within the narrow walls of his limited acquisitions. Therefore, if we want to gain freedom and happiness, we must embrace all by giving up the self.

However, when the self is given up, the giver is still there, for the act of giving is only possible when there is one who gives and the other who is given. However further we may go, there always remains the giver that does the act of giving. As long as there is an idea of giving somewhere in one's consciousness, the giving agent will always be left behind as an insoluble residue, and no final giving up of the self will be possible. If one wants to be an absolute giver, one must altogether transcend the dualism of one who gives and the other who is given. When this is accomplished, there takes place the entire shifting of positions, and one who gives is at once one who is given. The absolute *transference* from ME to the NOT ME is at once the *transference* (*parinamana: eko*)[2] from the NOT ME to ME. Here, one has entered the spiritual world—the

[2] See Chapter IV, 3.

Kingdom of Faith. The key to unlock the mysteries of this Kingdom is *love*, for Faith is the highest culmination of love.

In love all the contradictions of existence merge themselves and are lost. In love are unity and duality not at variance. Love is one and two at the same time. In love, here I am and I am not; I am in thee and thou in me. In love, loss and gain are harmonized. The lover constantly gives himself up to gain himself in love. Indeed, love is what brings together and inseparably connects both the act of abandoning and that of receiving. Therefore, when a man loves, giving becomes a matter of joy to him, for he transcends the dualistic notion of one who gives and the other who is given. He transcends even the idea of giving. He gives and yet he gives not. For him, giving is at once being given.

Love is the perfection of consciousness. We do not love because we do not comprehend, or rather we do not comprehend because we do not love. For love is the ultimate meaning of everything around us. It is not a mere sentiment; it is truth; it is the joy that is at the root of all creation. It is the white light of Pure Feeling that emanates from Amida (Amitabha), the Infinite Light. So, to be at home one with this All-feeling Being, who is in the external sky, as well as in our inner heart, we must attain to that summit of consciousness, which is love. It is through the heightening of our consciousness into love, and extending it all over the world, that we can be *transferred back* into the Original Love, that we can attain communion with Amida, the Spirit of Joy (*Sambhoga-kaya*).

Nirvana (*nehan*) preached by Shakyamuni, the founder of Buddhism, is nothing else than this highest culmination of love. It is the absolute dying to the self, which is at once the absolute *rebirth* of the self in the Universal Self. It is the *extinction* of the lamp in the morning light. This is the true awakening or *enlighten-ment*. One has entered the spiritual world or the Kingdom of Faith. But he who has entered the Kingdom of Faith never sits in idleness in that country, for Faith is motion and rest in one; bondage and liberation are not antagonistic in Faith. He comes back to this world, and does not stop for a moment extending measureless love for all creatures, even as a mother for her only child, whom she protects with her own life. Up above, below, and all around him he extends his love, which is without bounds and obstacles, and which is free from all cruelty and antagonism. While standing, sitting, walking, lying down, even in his dreams, he keeps his mind active in this exercise of universal good-will.

3

According to history, Shakyamuni attained Enlightenment at Buddhagaya on the Nairanjana River more than twenty-five centuries ago, when he was thirty-five. In the *Saddharma-pundarika Sutra* (*The Lotus of the True Law*), however, Shakyamuni declares as follows: "In the immeasurably infinite past I attained *Bodhi* (Enlightenment), and I have been living here for an incalculably long period of time. I am immortal." This declaration comes from the deepest recesses of his nature where he and his audience and all of us essentially move and have their being. This is the Eternal *I am* that speaks through the *I am* that is in me. The finite I am has attained its perfect end by realizing its freedom of harmony in the Infinite *I am*: Here I am and I am not; Thou dwellest in me and I in Thee. This is the realm of true spirituality—Faith—where the eye with which I see Amida is the same with which Amida sees me. This is the state of absolute freedom where the self permeates into all other selves through union with the Great Self. The finite I am finds its larger self in the whole world, and is filled with an absolute certainty that it is immortal. It must die in its enclosures of self, but it never can die where it is one with the All, for there is its truth, its joy.

However, by the process of knowledge we can never attain the oneness with the Infinite *I am*—the Universal Self. We can only *feel* Him through the immediate intuition of the *loving heart*. Knowledge is partial, because our knowledge is an instrument, it is only a part of us; it can give us information about things which can be divided and analyzed, and whose properties can be classified, part by part. But Amida, the Infinite Being, is perfect and eternal, and knowledge which is partial can never be a knowledge of Him. He can be known only through *pure feeling* for *pure feeling* is knowledge in its completeness, it is knowing by our whole being. Knowledge sets us apart from the things to be known, but *pure feeling* knows its object by fusion. Such knowledge is immediate and admits no doubt. It is the same as knowing our own selves, only more so. It transcends the dualism of the knower and the object known. When it is said to see something, this something is nothing else than itself.

This selfsame knowledge—*pure feeling*—which is unanalyzable into subject and object, into one who knows and that which is known, is none other than *Prajna* (*hannya*)—the *transcendental* spiritual intuition. *Prajna* is a knowledge that knows and yet knows not, an intuition that does not intuit, a thought that is not thought.

It is *no-thinking-ness* (*munen*) or *mind-less-ness* (*mushin*) not in the sense of unconsciousness, but in the sense that it transcends all traces of discursive or analytical understanding. All thinking involves the distinction of this and that, for thinking means to dichotomize, to divide, to analyze. *Prajna* or no-thinking-ness or mind-less-ness does not divide, but is *beyond* the self-centered mind (*vijnana*) which is the maker of the interminable complexities of discriminations and divisions. As the *basal pure feeling, Prajna* underlies and encompasses the ordinary, matter-of-fact, object-distinguishing, time-marking consciousness. The whole of the Buddhist teaching revolves about this central idea of *pure feeling* or *no-thinking-ness* or *mind-less-ness,* showing that no spiritual truth could be grasped by ratiocination or demonstration. This is not, however, the denial of understanding or the stoppage of reasoning, but the means to reach the root and foundation of sense and understanding. The ordinary object-distinguishing, time-marking consciousness will lose its way, if not awakened to and guided by the light of this *basal pure feeling* (*Prajna*), in the labyrinth of interminable complexities. *Prajna*'s all-illuminating light does not obliterate distinctions, but makes them stand out most clearly in their true, spiritual significance, for the self is now dead and all is seen reflected in the serene mirror of selflessness (*muga*). Being not one of the effects of our human endeavor, *Prajna* is the ground of our existence, that is, the *meta* (*beyond*)-*physical condition* on which our whole life of conduct and science rests. *Prajna* is, so to speak, a transparent eyeball which is free from all color and which, for this reason, discerns all colors. The opening of this kind of eye is enlightenment or the revelation of Amitabha, the Infinite Light. This is the luminous vision of the Pure Land (*Sukhavati: Jodo*) of Amida.

4

In the *Larger Sukhavati-vyuha Sutra* (*The Embellishment of the Pure Land*), Shakyamuni preaches to Ananda, one of his disciples, concerning the magnificence of the Pure Land (*Sukhavati*), Amida's World of Bliss, where He reigns since He attained Buddhahood ten *kalpas*[3] ago:

"Now,[4] O Ananda, that world called *Sukhavati* (Pure Land) belonging to that Buddha Amitabha is prosperous, rich, good to live in, fertile, lovely, and filled with many gods and men. . . . O Ananda, that world *Sukhavati* is fragrant with several sweet-smelling scents, rich in manifold flowers and fruits, adorned with gem trees, and frequented by tribes of manifold

[3] 1 *kalpa* = 432,000,000 years.
[4] From F. Max Müller's English translation in *The Sacred Books of the East*, Vol. XLIX. (My citations are slightly changed.) See Chapter IV, 1.

sweet-voiced birds, which have been made by that Buddha Amitabha on purpose. . . .

"There are lotus flowers there, half *yojana*[5] in circumference. There are others, one *yojana* in circumference; and others, two, three, four, or five *yojanas* in circumference; nay, there are some as much as ten *yojanas* in circumference. And from each gem-lotus there proceed thirty-six hundred thousand *kotis*[6] of rays of light. And from each ray of light there proceed thirty-six hundred thousand *kotis* of Buddhas, with bodies of golden color, who go and teach the Law of Truth (*Dharma*) to beings in the immeasurable and innumerable worlds in the eastern quarter. Thus also in the southern, western, and northern quarters, above and below, in the cardinal and intermediate points, they go

[5] 1 *yojana* = 9 miles.
[6] 1 *koti* = 10 millions.

their way to the immeasurable and innumerable worlds and teach the Law to beings in the whole world. . . .

"In that world *Sukhavati*, O Ananda, there flow different kinds of rivers; there are great rivers there, one *yojana* in breadth; there are rivers up to twenty, thirty, forty, fifty *yojanas* in breadth, and up to twelve *yojanas* in depth. All these rivers are delightful, carrying water of different sweet odor, carrying bunches of flowers adorned with various gems, resounding with sweet voices. And, O Ananda, there proceeds from an instrument which consists of hundred thousand *kotis* of parts, which embodies heavenly music and is played by clever people, the same delightful sound which proceeds from those great rivers, the sound which is deep, unknown, incomprehensible, clear, pleasant to the ear, touching the heart, beloved, sweet, delightful, never tiring, never disagreeable, pleasant to hear. . . .

"And again, O Ananda, the borders of those great rivers on both sides are filled with jewel trees of various scents, from which bunches of flowers, leaves, and branches of all kinds hang down. And if the beings who are on the borders of those rivers wish to enjoy sport full of heavenly delights, the water rises to the ankle only after they have stepped into the rivers, if they wish it to be so; or if they wish it, the water rises to their knees, to their hips, to their sides, and to their ears. And heavenly pleasures arise. Again if the beings then wish the water to be cold, it is cold; if they wish it to be hot, it is hot; if they wish it to be hot and cold, it is hot and cold, according to their pleasure. . . .

"And, O Ananda, there is nowhere in that *Sukhavati* world any sound of sin, obstacle, misfortune, distress, and destruction; there is nowhere any sound of pain, even the sound of perceiving what is neither pain nor pleasure is not there, O Ananda, how much less the sound of pain. For that reason, O Ananda, that world is called *Sukhavati* (Pure Land of Bliss), shortly, but not in full. For, O Ananda, the whole *kalpa* would come to an end, while the different causes of the pleasure of the world *Sukhavati* are being praised, and even then the end of those causes of happiness could not be reached. . . .

"And again, O Ananda, in that world *Sukhavati*, beings do not take food consisting of gross materials of gravy or molasses; but whatever food they desire, such food they perceive, as if it were taken, and become delightful in body and mind. Yet they need not put it into their mouth.

"And if after they are satisfied, they wish different kinds of perfumes, then with these very heavenly kinds of perfumes the whole Buddha Country is scented. And whosoever wishes to perceive there such perfume, every perfume of every scent of the Gandharvaraja does always reach his nose. . . .

"And again, O Ananda, in that Buddha Country whatever beings have been born, and are being born, and will be born, are always constant in Absolute Truth, till they have reached *Nirvana.* And why is that? Because there is no room or mention there of the other two divisions, such as beings not constant or constant in falsehood. . . .

"And again, O Ananda, in the ten quarters, and in each of them, in all the Buddha countries equal in number to the sand of the River Ganga, the blessed Buddhas equal in number to the sand of the Ganga glorify the Name[7] of the blessed Amitabha; they preach his Fame, they proclaim his Glory, they extol his Virtue. And why? Because all beings who

[7] See Chapter IV, 2.

hear the Names of the blessed Amitabha, and having heard it, raise their thought with joyful longing, even for once only, will not turn away again from the Highest Perfect Knowledge (Enlightenment). . . ."

The mythological representation of spiritual truth is an essential element in the organism of Shakyamuni's Teaching. When we read Buddhist *Sutras,* myth bursts in upon our ordinary consciousness with a revelation of something new and strange, and the narrow, matter-of-fact, workaday experience is suddenly flooded and transfused by the inrush of a vast experience, as from another world. The visions of the mythopoeic imagination are received by the self of ordinary consciousness with a strange surmise of the existence, in another world, of Another Self which, while it reveals itself in these visions, has a deep secret which it will not disclose.

Mythological expression represents natural products of that world of time-space-transcending *pure feeling* which encompasses the field of ordinary, matter-of-fact, time-space-consciousness in our minds. Shakyamuni appeals to that *major* and *basal* part of man's nature which is not articulate and logical, but *feels* and *wills* and *acts*—to that part which cannot explain what a thing is, or how it happens, but *feels* spontaneously that the thing is good or bad, and expresses itself, not scientifically in theoretic judgments, but practically in value-judgments—or rather value-feelings. In appealing, through the recital of dreams, to that major part of us which feels *values,* which wills and acts, Shakyamuni indeed goes down to the bedrock of human nature. At that depth man is more at one with Universal Nature—more in her secret, as it were—than he is at the level of his "higher" faculties, where he lives in a conceptual world of his own making which he is always endeavoring to think.

After all, however high man may rise as *thinker*, it is only of *values* that he genuinely thinks; and the ground of all values—the Value of Life—was already apprehended before the dawn of thinking, and is still apprehended independently of thinking. Why is life *worth* living? Why is it *good* to be here? The problem is not propounded to thought and thought cannot solve it. Thought can *feel* that it has been propounded and solved elsewhere, but cannot genuinely think it. It is propounded to the inmost depth of our nature, and is ever silently being understood and solved by that basal part of our self. And the most trustworthy, or least misleading report of what the problem is, and what its solution is, reaches consciousness through *feeling*. *Feeling* stands nearer than thought does to that *basal self* which is, indeed, at once the living problem of the Universe and its living solution.

Shakyamuni appeals from the world of the senses and the scientific understanding, which is too much with us, to this deep-lying part of human nature. The responses are not given in articulate language which the scientific understanding can interpret; they come as dreams, and must be received as dreams, without thought of doctrinal interpretation. Their ultimate meaning is the *feeling* which fills us in beholding them, and when we wake from them, we see our daily concerns and all things temporal with purged eyes.

The effect which Shakyamuni produces by myth in his discourses is produced, in various degrees, by Nature herself without the aid of literary or other art. The sense of majesty and sublimity which comes over us when we look into the depths of the starry sky, the sense of our own short time passing, with which we see the cherry flowers bloom again, these, and many like them, are natural experiences which closely resemble the effect produced in the hearer's mind by Shakyamuni's discourses. When these natural moods are experienced, we *feel* the Unthinkable Timeless Being that was, and is, and ever shall be, overshadowing us; and familiar things—the stars, and the cherry blooms—become suddenly strange and wonderful for our eyes are opened to see that they declare His presence. It is such moods of feeling in his hearer that Shakyamuni induces, satisfies, and regulates by Myth which sets forth the Timeless Being, the Universe, and Ideals in vision.

This *pure feeling*, which is experienced as solemn intuition of the overshadowing presence of the Unthinkable Timeless Being, appears in our ordinary object-distinguishing, time-marking consciousness, but does not originate in it. It is to be traced to the influence on consciousness of the persistence in us of that primeval condition from which we are sprung (*Nirvana*), when Life was still as sound asleep as Death, and there was no Time yet. It is natural, therefore, that we should fall for a while, now and then, from our waking, time-marking life, into the *timeless* slumber of this primeval life of *selflessness*; for the principle solely operative in that primeval life is indeed the fundamental principle of our nature, being that basal part of our self which, made from the first, and still silently in timeless slumber, makes the assumption on which our whole rational life of conduct and science rests—the assumption that life is *worth* living, that it is *good* to be here.

Man's anticipation of death would oppress his life with insupportable melancholy, were it not that his conscious life feels down with its roots into that *innermost* center of his nature which, without sense of past or future or self, silently holds on to life, in the *implicit*

---

faith that it is worth living—that there is a Cosmos in which it is good to live. As it is, there is still room enough for melancholy in his hours of ease and leisure. If comfort comes to him in such hours, it is not from his thinking out some solution of his melancholy, but from putting out his thought, and sinking alone into the timeless slumber of that fundamental part of his self. When he wakes into daily life again, it is with the elementary faith of this basal part of his self, newly confirmed in his heart; and he is ready, in the strength of it, in fearlessness, to defy all that seems to give it the lie in the world of sense and understanding. Sometimes, and more often, this immovable faith does not merely transfigure, but dispels the very melancholy which overclouds him at the thought of death, and fills his heart with *sweet hope* of personal immortality.

To sum up, *pure feeling* is at once the solemn *intuitions* of the Unthinkable Timeless Being overshad-

---

owing us and the *faith* that life is good. In the first phase, *pure feeling* appears as an abnormal experience of our conscious life, as a well-marked ecstatic state; in its other phase as the faith that life is good, *pure feeling* may be said to be a normal experience of our conscious life: it is not an experience occasionally cropping up alongside of other experiences, but a feeling which accompanies all the experiences of our conscious life—that *sweet hope*, in the strength of which we take the trouble to seek after the particular achievements which make up the waking life of conduct and science. Such feeling, though normal, is rightly called *transcendental*, because it is not one of the effects, but the *condition* of our entering upon and persevering in the course of endeavor which makes experience.

In the wide-awake life of conduct and science, understanding, left to itself, claims to be the measure of truth; sense, to be the criterion of good and bad.

Pure feeling, welling up from another part of the self, whispers to understanding and sense that they are leaving out something. What? Nothing less than the *unthinkable* plan of the Universe. And what is that unthinkable plan? The other part of the self indeed comprehends it in silence *as it is*, but can explain it to the understanding only in the symbolical language of imagination—in vision.

It is in *pure feeling*, manifested normally as faith in the Value of Life, and ecstatically as intuition of the Unthinkable Timeless Being, and not in thought proceeding by way of speculative construction, that consciousness comes nearest to the object of metaphysics: Ultimate Reality, because, without that faith in the Value of Life, thought could not stir. It is in *pure feeling* that consciousness is aware of The Good, or the Universe as a place in which it is *good* to be. *Pure feeling* is thus the beginning of metaphysics, for metaphysics cannot make a start without assuming The Good; but it is also the end of metaphysics, for speculative thought does not really carry us farther than the *feeling*, which inspired it from the first, has already brought us: we end as we began, with the feeling that it is good to be here.

II

The Essence of Goodness

1

Shinshu[1] or the True Religion is, as the name indicates, a religion founded upon Truth. Within us we have a *hope* which always walks in front of our narrow experience; it is the undying *faith* in the *deepest truth* in us. Facts are many, but *truth* is *one*, and to find out the One is to possess the All. Through all the diversities of the world, the *one* in us is ever seeking unity—unity in knowledge, unity in love, unity in purposes of will, and

[1] The literal meaning of the Japanese word *Shinshu* is "True (*Shin*) Religion (*shu*)."

its highest joy is when it reaches the One in all within its Eternal Unity. Were it not that the deeper roots of our nature find their permanent soil in the One Central Truth, then our consciousness would ever be restricted only to the immediate vicinity of the narrow present, and we would miss our inner perspective; then all opposites would ever remain opposites, and we could never find an *inner medium* through which our differences could ever tend to meet; then we could have no understanding, no blending of hearts, no cooperation in life.

Man is more in *truth* than he is in *fact.* Essentially, we are *spirit.* We belong not to this world, in so far as our sense and our understanding now show us this world. We even now belong to a higher and richer realm than this. Therefore, we have a feeling that we are much more than at present we seem to be, that the state not yet experienced by us is more *real* and *true* than that under our direct experience. Who amongst us conceives himself except as the remote goal of some ideal process of coming to himself and of awakening to the truth about his own life? Who am I? No finite process of finding and defining can exhaust *my whole true meaning*. Our *real nature,* our *true self* is an elusive goal for any temporal search. It constitutes, so to speak, the genuinely and wholesomely *occult* aspect of our commonplace life. The gates seem barred whenever we try to penetrate this so familiar, and precious, and yet so occult world. It is a very precious secret which is beyond our human sense and understanding. It is the object of our *will,* but not of our sense nor yet of our abstract thought; of our *love,* but not of our verbal confession, and however sense deceives, and however ill thought defines, we remain *faithful* to the ideal of it.

As we have this feeling for our *future self* which is outside our present consciousness, so we have a feeling for our *greater self* which is outside the limits of our personality. There is no man who has not this feeling to some extent, ever sacrificed his selfish desire for the sake of some other person, who has never felt a pleasure in undergoing some loss or trouble because it pleased somebody else. It is a truth that man is not a detached being, that he has a *universal* aspect. Our roots must go deep down into the Universal to attain the greatness of personality. If we were made to live in a world where our own self was the only factor to consider, then that would be the worst prison imaginable to us, for our deepest joy is in growing greater and greater by more and more union with the all. This, however, would be an impossibility, if we were not linked by the ties of a law *common to all*, and deeper and truer than that of necessity. Only by awakening to this One Universal Law (*Dharma*)—the *implicit truth* of all things, the *ultimate purpose* working within our self—

and by following it, do we become great, do we realize the *universal life.* It is the function of *religion* not to destroy our inmost purpose, but to fulfill it. As the child in its mother's womb gets its sustenance through the union of its life with the larger life of its mother, so our self is nourished only through the recognition of its inner kinship with the Eternal, through its communication with the Infinite, by which it is surrounded and fed, whereas our self is obscured by work done by the compulsion of self-centered desire or fear. In truth we are not sundered beings. We are correlated one to another in the *deepest harmony* that exists between us and our fellow beings. Our love of life is really our *will* to continue our relation with the all, with the whole world. It is that *goodwill* or *love's will* which does its work in the depths of the social being. It is the will for the good of the society. It is love's will. It transcends the limits of the present and the personal. It is on the side of the Infinite, of the Universal. As the mother reveals *herself* in the service of her children, so our freedom is not freedom from action, but freedom in action, which can only be attained in the work of love. The emancipation of our self is in realizing *goodwill* and *love*. This is what Shakyamuni describes as *extinction* (*Nirvana*) — the extinction of selfishness.

When the self-centered mind in us chafes against the Universal Law, we become morally small and must suffer. In such a self-centered life, we always live behind barricades, and our homes are not real homes, but artificial barriers around us. It is our life of the self that creates divisions and disunion everywhere and gives rise to miseries of all kinds. Yet we complain that we are not happy, as if miseries were not of our own making. Amida, the Universal Spirit, is waiting to deliver us from this prison-house of misery and suffering and to crown us with happiness, but our enveloped self would not accept it.

Our lust, our greed, our desire of comfort result in cheapening man to his lowest value. He gets his sole value from being useful; he is made into a machine and is defined by the market value of the service we can expect of him. It is self-deception on a large scale. Our desires blind us to the *truth* that is in man, and this is the greatest wrong done by ourselves to our own humanity. It deadens our consciousness, and is but a gradual method of spiritual suicide. But when by *love* we know him as a *spirit,* we know him as our own. We at once feel that cruelty to him is cruelty to ourselves, to make him small is stealing from, and humiliating our own humanity.

Therefore, if we want to live a real and true life, we have to surrender our self-power to the Universal Power, and to realize that it is our own power. The

Universal Power which is manifested in the Universal Law (*Dharma*) is in truth one with our own power. Really there is no limit to our powers, for we are not outside the Universal Power which is the expression of the Universal Law. The same energy which vibrates and passes into endless forms of the world manifests in our inner being as *wisdom,* and there is no break in unity. It is our *ignorance* which makes us think that our self, as self, is real, that it has its complete meaning in itself. When we take this wrong view of self, then we try to live in such a manner as to make self the ultimate object of our life. Then are we doomed to disappointment like the man who tries to reach his destination by firmly clutching the dust of the road. Our self has no means of holding us, for its own *nature* is to transcend itself, to realize the *ultimate meaning* (*dharma*) of itself. Therein lies man's freedom—the *naturalness* (*jinen*), as Shinran, the founder of the True Religion (*Shinshu*), puts it.

At first sight it seems that man counts that as freedom by which he gets unbounded opportunities of self-gratification and self-aggrandizement. But surely this is not borne out by history. Our revelatory men have always been those who have lived the life of self-sacrifice. The higher nature in man always seeks for something which transcends itself and yet is its deepest truth; which claims all its sacrifice, yet makes this sacrifice its own recompense. This is man's *dharma,* man's *religion,* and man's self is to carry this sacrifice to the altar.

We can look at our self in its two different aspects. The self which displays itself, and the self which transcends itself, and thereby *reveals* its own meaning. To display itself it tries to be big, to stand upon the pedestal of its accumulations, and to retain everything to itself. To reveal itself it gives up everything it has, thus becoming perfect like a flower that has blossomed out from the bud.

The lamp contains its oil, which it holds securely in its close grasp and guards from the least loss. Thus is it *separate* from all other objects around it and is miserly. But when lit, it finds its meaning at once; its relation with all things far and near is established, and it freely sacrifices its fund of oil to feed the flame.

Such a lamp is our self. So long as it hoards its possessions it keeps itself dark, its conduct contradicts its *true purpose*. When it finds illumination it forgets itself in a moment, holds the light high, and serves it with everything it has; for therein is its *revelation*. This revelation is the freedom which Shakyamuni preached. He asked the lamp to give up its oil. But purposeless giving up is a still darker poverty which he never could have meant. The lamp must give up its oil to the light and thus set free the *implicit purpose* it has in its hoard-

ing. This is emancipation. The path Shakyamuni point-
ed out was not merely the practice of self-abnegation,
but the widening of *love*. Therein lies the *true* meaning
of Buddhism.

The naturalness (*jinen*) which Shinran
preached is nothing less than this emancipation of the
self; a holy freedom through the melting of our self-
power (*jiriki*) in the Other Power (*tariki*), through the
surrender of our self-will (*hakarai*) to the Eternal Will;
a familiarity with Amida—the Infinite Light. This is
what Shinran meant by declaring that the direct road
to deliverance is *absolute faith* in Amida.

2

Religious faith is, it is hardly necessary to say,
not a mere self-complacent belief. It wants to be confirmed by the Teaching. Merely to say, "I believe," is not

sufficient; "I believe" must be confirmed by doctrinal authority. If my faith is true, it must be confirmed by the Teaching of the Enlightened One; and if his Teaching is really true besides being invested with traditional authority, it must be confirmed by my inner experience. If there should be a collision between faith and doctrine, this would mean: faith lacks in solid foundation and permanent value, being a temporary kindling of soul-fire; or doctrine has no element whatever of validity and eternity in it, the authority conventionally ascribed to it being merely formal and superficial. When both of them are genuine, there is perfect harmony between them and they are confirmatory each to the other. Both testify the One Eternal Truth.

Shinran (1173-1263), the founder of *Shinshu*, sought the confirmation of his faith in the Teaching of Shakyamuni. In fact, the *Kyo-gyo-shin-sho* (*Doctrine-*

Practice-Faith-Attainment), the fundamental textbook of *Shinshu*, which was written by Shinran, is a collection of one hundred and forty-three passages culled from twenty-one *Sutras* in which Shinran found his faith thoroughly confirmed. Moreover, its confirmation was also in the teaching of his teacher Honen himself. In the *Tanni-sho* (*Tract on Deploring the Heterodoxies*) compiled by Yuienbo, one of his disciples, Shinran declares:

"As far as I, Shinran, am concerned, I have no other alternative than believing what my teacher taught me: 'Leave your deliverance with Amida, uttering the *Nembutsu*[2] with singleness of heart.' Whether the

---

[2] *Nembutsu* (*Buddha-anusmriti* in Sanskrit) means literally "thinking of (*nen: anusmriti*) the Buddha (*butsu: Buddha*)." But it has come to be synonymous with *shomyo* or "reciting or uttering (*sho*) the Name (*myo*)." To the followers of the Shin Teaching of Buddhism, *nembutsu* means to think of or to recollect the Eternal Love's Will of Amida Buddha by uttering His Name: *Namu-Amida-Butsu*! See Chapter IV, 2, 3.

Nembutsu is truly the cause of my being born in the Pure Land or whether it is the act that will carry me down to hell, I wholly know nothing about that. Even if I were cheated by Honen Shonin, and were to go to hell because of practicing the *Nembutsu*, I have no regret at all in me. The reason is: If I, being capable of attaining Buddhahood by striving in practice other than the *Nembutsu*, were to go to hell because of uttering the *Nembutsu*, then there could well be a ground for me to regret that I was cheated; but in truth any practice is beyond my power, and so hell will be my ultimate abode anyway. If the Original Vow[3] of Amida is true, the teaching of Shakyamuni Buddha cannot be untrue. If the teaching of Shakyamuni Buddha is true, the expositions by Zendo[4] cannot be untrue. If Zendo's exposi-

[3] It means Amida's Eternal Saving Will to deliver all beings from this world of misery and suffering and have them born in his Buddha Country—the Pure Land. See Chapter IV.
[4] See Chapter IV, 3.

tions are true, how could it be that what Honen taught me was untrue? If Honen's teaching is true may I not say that what I, Shinran, say is also not untrue? After all, such is my humble *faith*. However, it is entirely up to you whether you take up the *Nembutsu* and put faith in it or cast it away."

In this we see how the inmost spiritual experience of Shinran is harmonized not only with the Teaching of Shakyamuni but with that of his own teacher Honen. When doctrine ceases to be regarded as something external to one's inner experience, it becomes at once the living principle of conduct; and when conduct is released from constraint or obstruction and becomes the *free* and *natural* movement of the spirit, joy expresses itself through everyday work.

In *Shinshu* the following Three *Sutras* are regarded as the primary source of its teaching.

(1) *The Larger Sukhavati-vyuha Sutra* (*The Embellishment of the Pure Land*). In this *Sutra* is recorded the discourse delivered by Shakyamuni at Gridhrakuta (Mount of Holy Vulture) in Rajagriha for the benefit of Ananda and Maitreya concerning the magnificence of the Pure Land of Amida and His Original Vow to save all beings. The *Sutra* was translated into Chinese by Sanghavarman in A.D. 252. The Chinese text is titled *Dai-muryoju-kyo* (*On the Eternal Life*).

(2) The *Amitayur-dhyana Sutra* (*Meditation on the Eternal Life*). It records Shakyamuni's sermon at the Royal Palace in Rajagriha, which was delivered so as to enlighten Ananda and Queen Vaidehi concerning the possibility for all beings to be born in the Pure Land and to attain Eternal Life. It was translated into Chinese by Kalayasa in A.D. 424. The title of the Chinese text is *Kan-muryoju-kyo* (*Meditation on the Eternal Life*).

(3) *The Smaller Sukhavati-vyuha Sutra.* It records what Shakyamuni preached to Shariputra at the garden of Anathapindada, Shravasti, concerning the Pure Land of Bliss and the wonderful Virtues of Amida. Kumarajiva translated it into Chinese in A.D. 402. *Amida-kyo* (*On Amida*) is the title of the Chinese text.

There were many Indian, Chinese, and Japanese predecessors of Shinran, who like him expounded the True (*Shin*) Teaching of deliverance by faith, and of these, *Shinshu* regards the following Seven Fathers as most contributing to the development of its doctrine: Ryuju (Nagarjuna, 150-250) and Tenjin (Vasubandhu, 320-400) in India, Donran (T'an-luan, 476-542), Doshaku (Tao-ch'o, 562-645), and Zendo (Shan-tao, 613-681) in China, and Genshin (942-1017) and Genku (1133-1212; more popularly known as Honen) in Japan.

III

The Revealer and the Redeemer

1

As we have seen already, when Shakyamuni meditated upon the way of releasing mankind from the grip of misery, he came to this truth: that when man attains his highest end by merging the individual in the Universal, he becomes free from the thralldom of pain. Let us consider this point more fully.

It cannot be said that we can find the Universal as we find other objects; there is no question of searching for him in one thing in preference to another, in one place instead of somewhere else. We do not have to run to the grocer's shop for our morning light; we open our eyes and there it is; so we need only give ourselves up to find that the Universal is everywhere.

So, our daily worship of Amida is not really the process of gradual acquisition of him, but the daily process of surrendering ourselves, removing all obstacles to union and extending our consciousness of him in devotion and service, in goodwill and love.

Thus to be conscious of being absolutely enveloped by Amida is not an act of mere concentration of mind. It must be the aim of the whole of our life. In all our thoughts and deeds we must be conscious of the Infinite. In all our actions let us feel that impetus of the Infinite Energy and be glad.

It may be said that the Infinite is beyond our attainment, so it is for us as if it were naught. Yes, if the word attainment implies any idea of possession, then it must be admitted that the Infinite is unattainable. But we must keep in mind that the highest enjoyment of man is not in the having, but in a getting, which is at the same time not getting. In all our deeper love getting and non-getting run ever parallel. The lover will say to his beloved: "I feel as if I have gazed upon the beauty of thy face from my birth, yet my eyes are hungry still; as if I have kept thee pressed to my heart for millions of years, yet my heart is not satisfied yet."

The tragedy of human life consists in our vain attempts to stretch the limits of things which can never become unlimited—to reach the Infinite by absurdly adding to the rungs of the ladder of the finite.

It is evident from this that the real desire of our heart is to get beyond all our possessions. The man truly realizes himself by outgrowing his possessions, and man's progress in the path of *eternal life* is through a series of renunciations.

That we cannot absolutely possess the Infinite Being is not a mere intellectual proposition. It has to be experienced, and this experience is bliss. The bird, while taking its flight in the sky, experiences at every beat of its wings that the sky is boundless, that its wings can never carry it beyond. Therein lies its joy. In the cage the sky is limited; it may be quite enough for all the purposes of the bird's life, only it is not more than is necessary. The bird cannot rejoice within the limits of the necessary. It must feel that what it has is immeasurably more than it ever can want or comprehend, and then only can it be glad. Thus our heart must soar in the Infinite, and she must feel every moment that in the sense of not being able to come to the end of her attainment is her supreme joy, her final freedom.

The finite pole of our existence has its place in the world of necessity. There man goes about searching for food to live, clothing to get warmth. In this region it is his function to get things. He is occupied with enlarging his possessions. But this act of getting is partial. To get is always to get partially, and it never can be otherwise. So this craving for acquisition belongs to our finite self.

But that side of our existence whose direction is towards the Infinite seeks not wealth, but freedom and joy. There the reign of necessity ceases, and there our function is not to get but to *be*. To be what? To be one with Amida. For the region of the Infinite is the region of *unity*. Words do not gather bulk when we know their meaning; they become *true* by being one with the idea. So man becomes true by being one with Amida.

But can it be then said that there is no difference between Amida and our individual self? Of course the difference is obvious. Amida is Amida, he is the infinite ideal of perfection. But we are not what we *truly* are; we are ever to *become* true, ever to become Amida. There is the eternal play of love in the relation between this *being* and *becoming*, and in the depth of this mystery is the Source of all truth that sustains the endless march of creation.

In the music of the rushing stream sounds the joyful assurance: "I shall become the sea." It is not a vain assumption; it is true humility, for it is the truth. The river has no other alternative. Though on both sides of its banks it has numerous fields and forests, villages and towns, which it can serve in various ways, it never can become a town or a forest. But it can and does become the sea. The lesser moving water has its affinity with the great motionless water of the ocean. It moves through the thousand objects on its onward course, and its motion finds its finality when it reaches the sea.

The river can become the sea, but she can never make the sea part and parcel of herself. If by some chance, she has encircled some broad sheet of water and pretends that she has made the sea a part of herself, we at once know that it is not so, that her current is still seeking rest in the great ocean to which it can never set boundaries.

In the same manner, our heart can only become Amida as the river can become the sea. Everything else she touches at one of her points, then leaves and moves on, but she never can leave Amida and move beyond him. Once our heart realizes her ultimate repose in Amida, all her movements acquire a purpose. It is this Ocean of infinite rest which gives significance to endless activities. It is this perfectness of *being* that lends to the imperfection of *becoming* that quality of beauty which finds its expression in all poetry, drama, and art.

There must be a complete idea that animates a poem. Every sentence of the poem touches that idea. When the reader realizes that pervading idea, as he reads on, then the reading of the poem is full of joy to him. Then every part of the poem becomes radiantly significant by the light of the whole. But if the poem goes on interminably, never expressing the idea of the whole, only throwing off disconnected images, however beautiful, it becomes wearisome and unprofitable in the extreme. The progress of our heart is like a perfect poem. It has an infinite idea which once realized makes all movements full of meaning and joy.

Man's cry is to reach his fullest expression. It is this desire for self-expression that leads him to seek power or wealth. But he has to discover that accumulation is not realization. It is the *inner light* that reveals him, not outer things. When this light is lighted, then in a moment he knows that man's highest revelation is Amida's own revelation in him. And his cry is for this— the manifestation of his heart, which is the manifestation of Amida in his heart. Man becomes perfect man, he attains his fullest expression, when his heart realizes itself in the Infinite Being who is Amida whose very essence is expression.

The real misery of man is in the fact that he has not fully come out, that he is self-obscured, lost in the midst of his own desires. The longing that rises up from his whole being is, therefore, the longing for the *perfect expression* of his self. This longing is more deeply inherent in man than his hunger and thirst for bodily sustenance, his lust for wealth and distinction. This prayer is not merely one born individually of him; it is in the depth of all things; it is the ceaseless *urging* in him of Amida, the Spirit of Eternal Manifestation.

The revealment of the Infinite in the finite, which is the motive of all creation, is not seen in such perfection in the starry heavens, in the beauty of flowers, as in the heart of man. For there *Will* seeks its manifestation in *will,* and freedom turns to win its final prize in the freedom of surrender.

Therefore it is the self of man which the Great Parent[1] of the Universe has left free. In his self man is free to disown his Parent. There our Amida must win his entrance. There he comes as a guest, not as the Parent, and therefore he has to wait till he is invited. There he comes to court our love. It is only in this region of will that anarchy is permitted; only in man's self that the discord of untruth and unrighteousness holds its reign; and things can come to such a pass that we may cry out in our anguish: "Such utter lawlessness could never prevail if there were a God!" Indeed, Amida has stood aside from our self, where his watchful patience knows no bounds, and where he never

---

[1] Parent or *Oya* in Japanese has no equivalent in English. It means either a father or a mother and also both of them as parents. Grammatically it has no gender, no number. It is neither "he" nor "she," it is either and both. It is difficult to find the proper pronoun for it. It is the one whose heart is wholly occupied with looking after its own children's welfare. It is probably

forces upon the doors if shut against him. For this self of ours has to attain its ultimate meaning, which is the *spirit* not through the compulsion of Amida's power, but through *love,* and thus become united with Amida in freedom.

When a man's spirit has been made one with Amida, when the Self-revealing One reveals Himself in the serene depth of his heart, then the consciousness of the Infinite becomes at once direct and *natural* to it as the light is to the flame. All the conflicts and contradictions of life are reconciled; knowledge, love, and action harmonized; pleasure and pain, enjoyment and renunciation become one in *naturalness;* the breach

more motherly than fatherly in that it is not the mighty master or head of a family who reproves, chastens, and punishes, but all-embracing love. This word, *oya,* is used as the title to Amida by the *Shinshu* followers. Their conception of Amida as Redeemer is that of the *oya,* not that of a mighty god who gives the sentence of everlasting damnation. See Chapter V, 2.

between the finite and the Infinite fills with love and overflows. The touch of an infinite mystery passes over the trivial and the familiar, making it break out into ineffable music. The trees and the stars and the blue hills appear to us as symbols aching with a meaning which can never be uttered in words. Every moment carries its message of the Eternal. Everything has eternal life and is a personality when it is touched by the spirit, when it is a spiritual revelation. The Formless appears to us in the form of the flower, of the fruit, or of the blue sky. The Boundless takes us up in his arms as a father and walks by our side as a friend.

Thus wherever the spirit moves, there is life, there is a Person. The Formless, the Eternal, the Boundless, the Universal, the Infinite is thus personified as the Supreme Person. Amida is such a personification in the enlightened spiritual consciousness of Shakyamuni. The formless Essential Law (*Dharmakaya*:

hosshin) which is beyond description and without attributes, revealed itself as Amida, the Spirit of Joy (*Sambhogakaya: juyushin* or *hojin*), in the enlightened consciousness of Shakyamuni, the Human Buddha (*Nirmanakaya: keshin* or *ojin*).

Amida is the Supreme Spirit from whom all spiritual revelations grow and to whom all personalities are related. Amida is at once the Infinite Light (*Amitabha*) and the Eternal Life (*Amitayus*). He is at once the Great Wisdom (*Mahaprajna: daichi*)—the Infinite Light—and the Great Compassion (*Mahakaruna: daihi*)—the Eternal Life. The Great Compassion is creator while the Great Wisdom contemplates. On the one hand Amida is creating, on the other he is perfection. In the one aspect he is essence, in the other, manifestation— both together at the same time, as is the song and the act of singing. Amida-consciousness which is the Eternal and Perfect Consciousness, comprehends in one glance, or *at once* the events of a billion years, and it is this infinite repose of Perfection whence the endless activities of the Universe are gaining their equilibrium every moment in absolute fitness and harmony.

The key to this Perfect Consciousness, to this Cosmic Consciousness, is in the spirit—the *world-man* we have in us—who is immortal, who is not afraid of death or suffering, who knows by a direct and immediate intuition—pure feeling—his inner kinship with the Universal Spirit by whom he is embraced and fed. To know our spirit apart from the self is the first step towards the realization of the supreme *deliverance* (*mukti*: *gedatsu*). We must know with absolute certainty that essentially we are spirit. This we can do by self-offering and love, for in love, I repeat, the sense of difference is obliterated and the human heart fulfills its *inherent purpose* in perfection, transcending the limits of itself and reaching across the threshold of the spirit-world.

Our great revealer Shakyamuni made manifest the true meaning of man's nature by giving up self for the love of mankind. He lived the life of the spirit, not of the self, and thus he proved to us the ultimate truth of humanity. Simple in wants, pure in heart, he took up all the responsibilities of life in a disinterested largeness of spirit. He had his *rebirth* from the blind envelopment of self to the freedom of true spirituality, where the finite *I am* is at one with the Eternal *I am,* where I am in Thee and Thou in me. Hence his declaration: "In the immeasurable infinite past I attained Enlightenment. I am immortal." Or, "Heavens above, heavens below, I alone am the Honored One."

2

The teachings taught by Shakyamuni, the Human Buddha, throughout his fifty years of missionary activity after his Enlightenment are no doubt the expression of the spiritual truth reflected in the serene mirror of his enlightened consciousness. He expounded *Dharma* or the Essential Law in various ways, and his discourses may be divided into various categories, as most Buddhist scholars do, such as "true" and "provisional," or "real" and "temporal." But all of them must be regarded as expounding the inner meaning of his spiritual consciousness. Some of the *Sutras* lay emphasis on "Thou" as revealed in the enlightened consciousness of the Human Buddha, some others are more concerned with the "I" phase of his spiritual consciousness, and still others with the interfusion of "I" and "Thou."

Shinran, the founder of *Shinshu* (True Religion), found the *Dai-muryoju-Kyo* (*Larger Sukhavati-vyuha Sutra*) to be the "true" teaching of Shakyamuni in its strictest sense, for the religious meaning of the interfusion of "I" and "Thou" is treated definitely and most sufficiently in this *Sutra*. In his principal work, the *Kyo-gyo-shin-sho* (*Doctrine-Practice-Faith-Attainment*), Shinran says: "Now, if I am to disclose the True Teaching, I must say it is none other than the *Dai-muryoju-kyo* (*Larger Sukhavati-vyuha Sutra*). The essential meaning of this *Sutra* is that Amida made the Vow,[2] opened widely the Treasury of *Dharma*, and having compassion on the ignorant and lowly, he selected out and bestowed the Jewels of Bliss upon them; while Shakyamuni, coming into this world, illuminatingly expounded the Way of Truth, as he wished to save all beings and bless them with the true benefit. Thus to reveal the Original Vow[3] of Amida is the purport of this

[2] See Chapter IV.
[3] See Chapter IV, 2.

Sutra. To wit, the Holy Name of Amida Buddha constitutes the main body of this *Sutra.*"

In the passage just quoted, Shinran refers to Amida as "Thou" revealed in the enlightened consciousness of Shakyamuni, and to Shakyamuni as the revelatory "I." While Amida, as "Thou," is working eternally as the Redeemer of the world, "I," the Revealer Shakyamuni, assumes an all-comprehensive compassionate attitude towards all beings and he himself becomes the Savior. Amida, the Savior, is thus entirely hidden and concealed behind Shakyamuni, the Revealer, and it takes the eye of the spirit to discern him existing in his "Thouness" in the selfsame spiritual consciousness of the Revealer. Even Ananda, one of the most favored disciples of Shakyamuni, could not realize the presence of Amida, "Thou," in the enlightened selfsame consciousness of his Teacher until he participated in the assembly on the Mount of Holy Vulture, where the Teacher revealed the secrets of the *Larger Sukhavati-vyuha Sutra*. Then it was that Ananda happened to see Amida revealing himself all of a sudden with his glory shining forth in its original grandeur through the person of Shakyamuni, the Enlightened One. In the *Kyo-gyo-shin-sho* (*Doctrine-Practice-Faith-Attainment*), Shinran quotes from the *Sutra*:

"Ananda said to the Buddha Shakyamuni: 'O World-honored One! Today your organs of sense look so pleased, the color of your skin is so pure, and your face so august; this may be likened to a transparent mirror whose reflections penetrate to the back of the mirror. Your majestic form, bright and illuminating, infinitely surpasses all others. Such an extraordinary grandeur as I see today I have never observed in you. O really it is, O Great Sage! This thought occurs to me that our World-honored One dwell today in the most excellent Truth, that you World-hero dwell today in the abode of a Buddha, that you World's Eye dwell today in the Walk of the Leader, that you World-lord dwell today in the All-surpassing Path, that you Heaven-honored One practice today the Virtues of a *Tathagata* (*Nyorai*).[4] All the Buddhas of the past, future, and present contemplate one another. How could it be that you, the present Buddha, are not contemplating all the Buddhas? How does it happen that your awe-inspiring splendor shines so illuminatingly today?'

---

[4] *Tathagata* (in Skt.) or *Nyorai* (in Jpn.) is an epithet of a Buddha, esp. of Amida Buddha. *Tatha* (*nyo*) means "thus," and *agata* (*rai*) "has come" or "has arrived." Hence, the *Tathagata* (*Nyorai*) is the "One who has thus come." On the other hand, *tathagata* can be divided also into *tatha* (*nyo*): "thus," and *gata* (*ko*): "gone" or "departed." Hence, the *Tathagata* has the meaning of *Nyoko* or the "One who has thus gone." No doubt the *tatha* is connected with the Mahayana conception of the Ultimate Truth as *Tathata* (Suchness or Thusness or Oneness). Therefore, the *Tathagata* is the "One who has the nature of *thusness* or *oneness in his coming from, and going back to the One True World.*"

"Thereupon, the World-honored One said to Ananda: 'How comes your question, O Ananda? Did the Heavens tell you to come and ask me about this? Or do you ask me, through your own wisdom, about my august countenance?'

"Ananda said to the Buddha: 'No Heavens have ever come to me to suggest this question. It is only from what I have seen that I ask this.'

"The Buddha said: 'Excellent, O Ananda! What you ask pleases me much. With the deepest wisdom awakened in you, with the subtlest eloquence, and out of compassion towards all beings, you have raised this wise question. The *Tathagata* in his Boundless Compassion feels with the whole universe. The reason why He is come out in this world is to make the Way of Truth shine out, to save all beings, and to bestow the true benefit on them. It is very difficult to meet and see a *Tathagata* who appears into this world only once in innumerable *kalpas*, just as it is very hard to see an udumbara-flower which blooms on a most rare occasion. What you ask now contains much benefit and enlightens all the Heavens and men. Know, O Ananda, that the Enlightenment attained by the *Tathagata* is far beyond understanding. It is the great guiding Light. His Wisdom is all-pervasive and knows no bounds and obstacles.'"

That Shinran took special care in quoting these passages from the *Dai-muryoju-kyo* (*Larger Sukhavati-vyuha Sutra*) conclusively proves that the basis of *Shinshu* is firmly laid upon the blending of "Thou" and "I" in the selfsame enlightened consciousness of Shakyamuni, the Human Buddha. The self-identity or the perfect interfusion of the Eternal *I am* and the finite *I am* is pictured in these passages by making Shakyamuni assume a divinely majestic appearance. Ananda penetrated into this mystery through his own spiritual insight. Shakyamuni was more than himself. His self was in complete communion with the All-feeling Universal Self. He was not himself; he was the Universal Self. It was this self-identity of I and Thou in his spiritual consciousness that enabled him to assume such a glorious appearance and to call himself "*Tathagata.*" And this selfsame spiritual consciousness of Shakyamuni deeply moved Ananda and made his mind reflect like a transparent eyeball what was going on in his Teacher's.

He whose spirit has been made one with Amida stands before man as the supreme flower of humanity. There man finds in truth what he is; for there the most perfect revelation of Amida is revealed to him in the spirit of man; for there we see the union of the Supreme Will with our will, our love with the Love Everlasting.

In Shakyamuni we see Amida's Wish fulfilled, the most difficult of all obstacles to His revealment removed, and Amida's own perfect Joy blossoming in humanity. Through him we find the whole world of man overspread with a divine homeliness. His life, burning with Amida's Love, makes all our earthly love resplendent. All the intimate associations of our life, all its experience of pleasure and pain, group themselves around this display of the Boundless Love, and form the drama that we witness in him.

IV

The Original Vow

1

According to the Myth told by Shakyamuni to Ananda in the *Dai-muryoju-kyo* (*Larger Sukhavati-vyuha Sutra*), long, long ago in the past, innumerable and more than innumerable and incomprehensible *kalpas* (aeons) ago, there was a Buddha, Lokeshvararaja by name. At that time there was a king who, having heard the sermon of this Buddha, felt a great joy in his heart and conceived a deep longing to seek Truth. He became a *bhikshu* (monk) and was called Dharmakara (Hozo). He excelled in knowledge; none were his equal. He called on Buddha Lokeshvararaja and said:

"O World-honored One! I have conceived in me a deep longing for *Bodhi*. I pray you will tell me all about the ways of Truth. I will practice them and realize a Buddha Country and embellish in the purest way this boundless and sublime Buddha Land. I wish I would attain Enlightenment at once in this world and do away with the roots of birth and death, of pain and sorrow."

Then Buddha Lokeshvararaja told the *bhikshu* all about the twenty-one billion Buddha-lands, what is good and what is not good of the beings thereof, and what is gross and what is refined in the lands, showing each as according to the wish of the *bhikshu*. Then, having listened to what Buddha Lokeshvararaja told and having seen all the excellences and sublimities of the Buddha-lands, the *bhikshu*, with his mind serene, with his will impartial, was absorbed in deep meditation for the space of five *kalpas*, to think out the pure and sublime ways to embellish his Buddha Country.

The end of the meditation having been attained, *bhikshu* Dharmakara selected out all the pure and untainted ways that had brought about the twenty-one billion wonderful Buddha-lands. Having performed the ways, he called on Buddha Lokeshvararaja and said: "I have already performed the pure and untainted ways to realize a sublime Buddha Land." Buddha Lokeshvararaja said to the *bhikshu*: "You should now tell what is in your mind, for it is now time. Let all the congregated here aspire to *Bodhi* and feel great joy. The *Bodhisattvas*,[1] hearing your words, will practice the Way, and will thereby fulfill their own innumerable vows."

[1] *Bodhisattva* (*bosatsu* in Jpn.) means a *sentient being* (*sattva*) who strives not only to attain *Enlightenment* (*Bodhi*) himself but to make others attain it. As a *bodhisattva* feels with others and suffers their sufferings as his own, he does not attain Enlightenment until his fellow-beings attain it.

Then *bhikshu* Dharmakara made, in the presence of Buddha Lokeshvararaja and before, as witness-
es, all the celestial beings, evil spirits, and all other
beings, *Forty-Eight* unsurpassed vows. These vows are
what is called the "Original Vow" (*Purva-pranidhana:
Hongan*) of *Bodhisattva* Dharmakara. Among the forty-
eight Vows, the most important one is the Eighteenth
Vow, which is as follows:

"When I have attained Buddhahood, if all
beings in the ten quarters, trusting in me with the most
sincere heart, should wish to be born in my Country,
and should utter my Name one to ten times, and if they
should not be born there, may I not attain
Enlightenment."

Then, again, having made the Forty-Eight Vows,
Bodhisattva Dharmakara uttered these verses:

"I have made the all-surpassing Vows, by which I
will certainly attain the highest Way. If these Vows

should not be fulfilled, may I not attain Enlightenment.

"If I should not be the Great Giver for immeasurable *kalpas* so as to save all the poor and miserable, may I not attain Enlightenment.

"When I have attained the Way of Buddhahood, my Name shall be heard all over the ten quarters. If there should be one who might not hear my Name, may I not attain Enlightenment.

"May I become the Teacher of all the heavenly and earthly beings, having sought for the Highest Way by practicing the Holy Work with selflessness, deep and right meditation, and pure wisdom.

"My Unthinkable Power shall radiate its all-pervasive Light upon the innumerable worlds, destroy the darkness of defilement, and deliver all beings from pain and misery.

"Giving them the Eye of Wisdom, I will destroy the gloom of ignorance; closing all the evil paths I will lead them to the Gate of Goodness.

"When I have accomplished the Excellent Work, my Glorious Light shall shine so brilliantly over the ten quarters that the light of the sun and the moon shall fade away, and the stars of heaven shall become invisible.

"Opening the Treasury of *Dharma* for the sake of all beings, I will widely distribute the Jewels of Bliss among them; and in the midst of multitudes, I will constantly preach the *Dharma* as a lion roars.

"Having worshipped all the Buddhas, I will complete the deeds of virtue; having fulfilled the Vow and Wisdom, I will become the Hero of the Universe.

"Like Thou[2] who art possessed of the Unimpeded Wisdom which shines on everything, I

[2] Buddha Lokeshvararaja.

will also have the Boundless Power of Virtue and Wisdom.

"If my Vows are to be fulfilled, all the worlds shall shake to the bottom and the Heavens shall shower down the wonderful flowers."

As *Bodhisattva* Dharmakara finished to recite these verses, the whole earth shook in six different ways at once, and heaven sprinkled the wonderful flowers over the earth. Then there arose music spontaneously in heaven and tuned the following words of praise: "Thou wilt certainly attain the Highest Perfect Enlightenment."

Then, the myth further runs, having made the Vows, *Bodhisattva* Dharmakara devoted himself single-heartedly for the embellishment of the wondrous Land. The Buddha Land he brought into being was wide, expansive, and incomprehensibly unique, knowing no withering and no change.

For a period of innumerable, inconceivable, and inexpressible *kalpas* Dharmakara devoted himself to the performance of the duties of a *Bodhisattva*. For the good of and in the stead of all beings he practiced immeasurable virtues, never conceiving the idea of lust, anger, and malevolence. Perfect was he in perseverance. No pain disturbed him. He was serene in his meditation. Unimpeded was his wisdom. Untiring was his will. Ever seeking the Pure Truth, he benefited all beings. Where he wished to be born, there he was born. Countless were the beings who were taught by him, and they were peacefully established in the All-surpassing True Way.

Like the blue lotus would his mouth give out an odor pure and fragrant. All the pores of his body would emit the fragrance of sandalwood and this would spread to all the innumerable worlds. Right and serene was his mien, and inexpressibly wonderful was his figure. From his hands came about unendingly treasures: garments, meals, flowers, incenses, canopies, banners and other things for decoration. All these things surpassed those of celestial beings. And in all things he was free and unimpeded.

Thus he had obtained the command of all necessaries, after performing the duties of a *Bodhisattva*. In short, he had completed all the virtues belonging to the life of a *Bodhisattva*, which consists of the realization of Love (*Karuna*) and Wisdom (*Prajna*).

Has *Bodhisattva* Dharmakara already attained Buddhahood?—Ananda asks Shakyamuni—Has he already entered *Nirvana*? Or has he not yet attained Enlightenment? Is he even now still living?

Bodhisattva Dharmakara has—Shakyamuni answers Ananda—already attained Buddhahood and is now living in a western quarter ten billion countries distant from here. The world of that Buddha is called the "Pure Land of Peace and Happiness." Already some ten *kalpas* have passed since *Bodhisattva* Dharmakara attained Buddhahood. He is surrounded by innumerable *Bodhisattvas* and is in possession of the endless perfection of his Buddha Country. He is called the Buddha of Infinite Light (Amitabha), because the limit of his Light is beyond measurement. He is also called the Buddha of Eternal Life (Amitayus), because the length of his Life is altogether incalculable and immeasurable, so that even though all the innumerable beings of the ten quarters, having assembled in one place, may collect their thoughts on measuring the length of his Life for a period of a hundred thousand million *kalpas*, and try to know the length of his Life, still is it not possible to know the limit.

* * * *

The gift of Amida's Vow is that he will not attain Enlightenment until by his *enlightenment* all beings in the Universe are also enlightened, that is, born in his Buddha Country—the Pure Land. Amida is eternally working as the Redeemer to fulfill his Original Vow. He is Heart of our hearts. He is the All-feeling Compassionate Heart which feels the want of all other hearts to be its own want. By his many-sided activity, which radiates in all directions, is he fulfilling the *inherent want* of his different creatures. That *inmost will,* that *ultimate purpose* working in the depths of our hearts is his asking us to seek deliverance. Man's inmost longing is to become immortal, to attain *eternal life.* In this very longing of ours, Amida too longs. It is the Absolute and Eternal Life which possesses the True World and is that world, that inspires this very longing. Amida is the Eternal Saving Will, the eternally working Original Vow. On the other hand, however, and at the same time, Amida is the infinite repose of Perfection, for, according to the myth, ten *kalpas* have already rolled away since he attained the Highest Perfect Enlightenment. And as he has already attained Enlightenment, it follows that our Rebirth or Enlightenment has already been effected *in timeless time* simultaneously with his Enlightenment.

Yes, we must know that within us we have *that* where space and time cease to rule and where the links of cause and effect are merged in unity. In this eternal abode of the spirit, the revelation of Amida, the Supreme Spirit, is already complete. The True, the All-conscious, the Infinite is hidden in the depths of our consciousness. The union with the All-knowing is already accomplished in timeless time.

No one can seek for a truth beyond his present self, unless the seeker is already in his *inmost purpose* one with the Eternal Life in which all truth is expressed. This *oneness* of divine and of finite purpose is already completed in the *basal part* of our heart, so that Amida is immanent, is everywhere nigh to us, and is everywhere *meant* by us all. At any instant, what we consciously *intend*, in all our finite strivings, is oneness with Amida. A will satisfied has in Amida's Whole Life found its goal, and seeks no other. It is the whole world of past, present, and future, it is that *universal life* that our every moment of conscious life implies and seeks. Amida is our Whole True Life, in whom we live and move and have our being, and in him we triumph and attain—not amidst the blind desires of our momentary self, but in that which our strivings always *intend*, and *will* and *love*. Indeed we have not now at once both wholly and consciously present the *complete expression* of our own will, but this complete expression, with us and in essence in us really, even now, but not consciously present to us now, this Whole Will and Life of ours is Amida.

Amida, the Spirit of Joy, has made himself into two. Joy, whose other name is love, must by its nature have duality for its realization. When the singer has his inspiration, he makes himself into two; he has within him his other self as the hearer, and the outside audience is merely an extension of this other self of his. A father seeks his own other self in his loved son. It is joy—love—that creates this separation, in order to realize through the separation the union. Love is most free and at the same time most bound. If Amida were absolutely free, there would be no creation. Amida, the Infinite Being, has assumed unto himself the mystery of finitude. He has willingly set limits to his Will, and has given us mastery over the little world of our own. It is like a father's settling upon his son some allowance within the limit of which he is free to do what he likes.

Though it remains a portion of the father's own property, yet he frees it from the operation of his own will. The reason of it is that the will, which is love's will and therefore free, can have its joy only in a union with another free will. A lover must have two wills for the realization of his love, because the consummation of love is in harmony, the *harmony* between freedom and freedom.

From the fullness of Love, Amida has made himself into two. He has himself chosen this heart of ours as his loved one, as his other self, as his hearer. He has bound himself to man, and this blissful bond, this parentage of supreme love has already been completed in timeless time. And He who has been gained *in eternity* is now being pursued in time and space, in joys and sorrows, in this world and in the innumerable worlds beyond. Our heart, like a river, has attained the Ocean of her fulfillment at one end of her being, and at the other end she is ever attaining it; at one end it is eternal rest and completion, at the other it is incessant movement and change. When our heart is awakened to this, when she knows both ends as inseparably connected, then she knows this world as her own household by the right of knowing the Master of this world as her own *Parent* (*oya*).[3] She finds this world overspread with a divine homeliness, the Infinite Original Love manifesting in all things of this world. Then all her services become services of love, all the troubles and tribulations of life come to her as trials triumphantly borne to prove the strength of her love. She has unlocked the mysteries of the spiritual world.

However, I repeat, we cannot attain true spirituality by successive additions of knowledge acquired bit by bit. We cannot grow more and more into Amida.

[3] See Chapter III, Note 1.

He is the Absolute One, and there can be no more or less in him. The revelation of the Supreme Spirit within our individual heart is, as we have seen, already in a state of absolute completion. We cannot think of it as depending on our limited powers (*jiriki*) for its gradual construction. If our relation with Amida, the Supreme Spirit, were all a thing of our own making, how should we rely on it as true, and how should it lend us support?

2

Love spontaneously gives itself in endless gifts. But these gifts lose their fullest significance if through them we do not reach that Love, which is the giver. To do that, we must have love in our own heart. When we have love in our heart, a mere token is of permanent worth to us. For it is not for any special use. It is an end in itself; it is for our whole being. As a token of his Boundless Love for us, Amida gave us a gift—the truest of all gifts. He gave us his Blessed Name (*myogo*) so that, whenever we utter and hear his Name being uttered, we may recollect, with a deep longing, our union with him already accomplished in timeless time. It is his call to us; it is his seeking for love in us.

Namu-Amida-Butsu! It is in remembrance of the Original Vow of Amida and his Boundless Love for us that we recite his Blessed Name. It is to recollect that this island of isolation has already been bridged over by him, and that he has not forgotten us, and will save us even now. It is to give our self up, and absolutely and without doubting, to trust (*Namu*) Amida Buddha (*Amida-Butsu*).[4] Nay, it is not we that utter his Name,

---

[4] *Namu-amida-butsu* is the transliteration of the Sanskrit *namomitabhaya buddha* or *namomitayuse buddhaya*. *Namo* or *namas* means "adoration" or "salutation," and *amitabhaya* (or *amitayuse*) *buddha* means "to the Buddha of Infinite Light (or of Eternal Life)." So "adoration to the Buddha of Infinite Light (or of Eternal Life)" is

but it is Amida who speaks to himself. It is his own utterance breathed in his breath. In the *Anjin-ketsujo-sho* (*Tract on the Final Settlement of Peaceful Mind*) written by an anonymous follower of the Pure Land Teaching, we read:

"The *Nembutsu* means to *think of* (*nen*) Amida Buddha (*butsu*), and to think of the Buddha is to remember that the Buddha has by the Active Power of his Original Vow cut asunder for all beings the bonds whereby they are tied to birth-and-death, and that he has thus matured the condition for their Rebirth in the

the meaning of *Namu-amida-butsu*. But in the Shin Teaching of Buddhism the full form of *Namu-amida-butsu* is regarded as the Name of Amida Buddha, because in it is embodied his original Vow or his Eternal Love's Will to enlighten and deliver us from the night of ignorance. It is Amida Buddha (*Amida-butsu*) that causes us to trust or *have faith in* (*namu*) him as our Light and Life. *Namu* and *Amida-butsu* are therefore essentially inseparable, being the two aspects of the One Eternal Will. *Namu* is *Amida-butsu* and *Amida-butsu* is *namu*.

Recompensed Land[5] where once entered they would never retrograde. When thinking of this merit accomplished by the Buddha, we rely single-heartedly upon the Original Vow, our threefold activity of body, mouth, and mind is supported by the Buddha-substance and we are raised up to the state of Enlightenment which constitutes Buddhahood. Therefore, lay it well to heart that your being absorbed in the *Nembutsu,* that is, your uttering the Buddha's Name, or your worshipping him or your thinking of him, is not an act originating in yourselves, but it is doing the very act of Amida Buddha himself." Or again in another place of the same book we read: "The purport of all the Three *Sutras* [of the Pure Land school] is to manifest the significance of the Original Vow. To comprehend the Vow means to com-

[5] *The Recompensed Land* (*hodo*) means the Pure Land that has come out as the *recompense* (*ho*) for the fulfillment of the Vow.

prehend the Name, and to comprehend the Name is to comprehend that Amida Buddha, by bringing to maturity his Vow and Virtue in the stead of all beings, effected their Rebirth (*ojo*)[6] even prior to their actual attainment. What made up the substance of his Enlightenment was nothing less than the Rebirth of all beings in the ten quarters of the universe. For this reason, we who practice the *Nembutsu* should remember, each time we hear the Buddha's Name being uttered, that our Rebirth has already been completed, because the Name issues from the Enlightenment (Buddhahood) attained by *Bodhisattva* Dharmakara who vowed that he would not attain Enlightenment until all beings in the ten quarters attained Rebirth."

[6] *Ojo* means literally "to go (*o*)" and "to be born (*jo*)" in another world, that is, in the Pure Land of Amida. In the Shin Teaching, Rebirth (*ojo*) or *Nirvana* is used in the sense of Enlightenment. Rebirth and *Nirvana* and Enlightenment are synonyms.

3

Our Rebirth or Enlightenment has already been completed in timeless time. But because of our self-centered mind we are *ignorant* of this fact. Our self-centered dualistic mind creates the hard separateness of the self. It prevents our self from merging in the universal time and touching the fundamental unity. It makes the self our fetter by making us think that our self as self is real, that it is an end in itself. Thus fearful eddies are created round different centers—eddies of self-interest, of pride, of power. This causes us to lay up obstructions and strengthen all the time the hindrance of karma.

The original meaning of the term karma is "action" (*kri*), and an action or a deed, good or bad, brings its own result on the doer, and therefore karma is the *moral law of cause-effect* dominating human activity. Our miseries and sufferings are due to our being tied and bound with the iron chain of human activity running on unbroken from time immemorial. All of us, as soon as we are born, carry a heavy burden of the immense accumulations of past human activities. We are caught in the net of karma which we human beings have been weaving since the unknown past. We are karma. Karma is human life itself. The whole of human life is a prison, the bars of which it is impossible to break. When the appropriate conditions are matured, an event takes place, regardless of our will. Though all of us love peace, war breaks out against our will. Birth, age, disease, and death press upon all with an impartial severity which there is no mitigating and no avoiding. We are hedged in on all sides, within and without, with fetters of *causation* (*inga*), moral as well as physical, so that we cannot do anything according to our will or ideal. Even action from good will often yields bad results. It does not suffice for us to be sincere, nor to have good intentions. How much suffering we may cause to others without wishing it, or knowing it! We can do just as much harm through not knowing as through unkindness. Moreover, we cannot even absolutely control our own bodies or regulate our own desires. We cannot with all our efforts drag ourselves away from evil, or force ourselves into the path of virtue. The overwhelming power of karmic necessity impels us to leave undone the good that we would do, and to do the evil that we would not.

When we reflect upon this, we cannot but shudder at our *abysmal sinfulness*. Bound on all sides with fetters of karmic necessity, we find ourselves plunged headlong into an ever rotating whirlpool of sin. We are sinful. Human life is an abyss of sin.[7] Wherever we go,

[7] Sin in Buddhism is the darkness of ignorance (*avidya*), or, as the author states, "a dead shell of our narrow self." See Chapter I, 1.

sin follows us like our own shadow. It seems there is no way for us to be free from sin except by being deprived of life. But man is not animal. He is *conscious* of his sinfulness. We are constantly under the oppressive consciousness of our sinfulness, and this consciousness, this pang, points to the way of liberation. Just because we are conscious of ourselves and know to judge our deeds, we are permitted to have a glimpse into a realm where no such human judgement avails. Traditionally speaking, being merely sin-conscious may not be more than a state of contemplation, but in our heart we feel that this consciousness is far more deeply seated and rises out of our *inmost* self which is somehow related to something that transcends itself and yet is its deepest truth. Our struggle with sinful existence is urged by this *something*, by this *Unthinkable* Power. If it were not for this fact, we should have no pang, no struggle, no suffering, no affliction of any kind. Our sin-consciousness is thus always linked with the *urge*. Without this urge in the human heart there would be no sin-consciousness in us, and therefore we know that sinfulness is somehow related with sinlessness or purity. It is in fact *The Pure* that so persistently presses itself into the domain of sinfulness, making the latter feel, as it were, uneasy and annoyed. The very fact of our intense spiritual suffering is the promise that we can eventually rise above it. In spiritual suffering is symbolized the infinite possibility of perfection or purification, the eternal unfolding of joy.

Sin oppresses us all the time, yet all the time we feel the persistent urge to seek deliverance. This urge, this impulse, which issues from our inmost nature, from the Center of our being, manifests itself as the *Nembutsu*. The *Nembutsu* is the vessel *transferred* to us by Amida so as to enable us to cross over the turbulent sea of sinful existence to the other shore of bliss. This crossing over, this *transference* over there is, however, not at all a gradual process from one stage to another. The very moment we embark on the boat in absolute trust in Amida, we find ourselves on the other shore; there is no gradation, no scaled progression, but a *leap* (*ocho*),[8] an *abrupt transference*, a discrete continuity. For this *transference* (*parinamana: eko*) is the working of the Unthinkable Power—the Other Power (*tariki*)—not of the self-power (*jiriki*).

Zendo (Shan-tao, 613-681), one of the Seven Fathers of *Shinshu*, gives us an allegory about the *transference* in his commentary on the *Kanmuryoju-kyo* (*Amitayur-dhyana Sutra*) which is one of the Three *Sutras* establishing the Teaching of *Shinshu*.

There was once a traveler going westwards across a vast desert. It was a lonesome journey. One day

[8] *Ocho* literally means "leaping (*cho*) crosswise (*o*)."

he heard a great noise far behind him and saw a band of robbers and a pack of wild beasts pursuing after him. Immediately he ran straight onwards with might and main to escape from the danger. But alas! there was a river across his way. It measured about a hundred paces in width and was divided into two streams by a narrow, white path, four or five inches wide—one on the right (northern) being a bottomless, turbulent stream of water, and the other on the left (southern) a boundless blazing stream of fire. It seemed quite a perilous undertaking to walk along this narrow, white path licked by the fire and washed by the water all the time. In the meantime, the robbers and the wild beasts were almost overtaking him. He was in utter despair, for he could neither advance, nor stop, nor retreat, without encountering the danger of death. But at the last moment, this thought hashed across his mind: "If I turn back, the robbers will surely fall upon me; even if I could escape from them, the beasts would not let me alone. And if I venture onwards, how could I escape from being swallowed up either by the water or the fire? Death encompasses me on all sides. My end is come anyway. Why not then boldly move forwards?" When thus finally he made up his mind, he heard a voice in the east: "Go straight along that path with a firm resolution, for it is the only way for you to escape from death." Then another voice came from the other shore: "With right thought and singleness of heart, straightway come hither to me. Don't be afraid of being drowned in the fire or the water, for I will protect you against the peril." Infinitely encouraged by these voices, he resolutely proceeded along the white path and instantly reached in safety the western shore. He was now in the Land of Bliss where he enjoyed the happiest and peaceful life of universal brotherhood.

What does this story mean? The traveler means us. This shore represents human life bound with the unbroken chain of karmic necessity, the other shore the spiritual world of the everlasting joy, of the absolute freedom from the karma-bondage. The river means our abysmal sinfulness, the turbulent water and the blazing fire representing greediness and cruelty in which the human mind is so much steeped. The voice that came from this shore represents the Teaching of Shakyamuni, and the voice from the other shore means the Great Compassionate Heart or the Original Vow of Amida. The white path is the *Nembutsu*—Amida's gift to us, the truest of all gifts. When we come to realize that we, karma-bound human beings, have no good conduct to rely upon on our side, and when we become fully conscious of our heinous sinfulness, the *Nembutsu* will rise of itself from the depths of our heart and we shall be instantly taken across to the other shore of deliverance. What keeps us on this side of the bridge so mercifully constructed by Amida's Boundless Compassion is our self-will (*hakarai*) and doubt. Unless these are removed, Amida's call will never rise upon our ear. Unconditional faith in the Great Compassion—absolute passivity or absolute surrender to the Other Power—is the only direct and the safest path leading to our Rebirth in the Pure Land.

In the *Tanni-sho* (*Tract on Deploring the Heterodoxies*), Shinran declares:

"Even the virtuous get born in the Pure Land. Why not we who are sinful? But people always say: 'Even the sinful get born in the Pure Land. Why not the virtuous?' This at first sight seems right, but it goes against the purport of the Original Vow, of the Other Power. The reason thereof is that those who undertake to do good by relying on their self-power (*jiriki*) lack that singleness of heart with which to trust upon the

Other Power (*tariki*), and this does not go in accord with the purport of Amida's Original Vow. But when one casts off the self-centered mind and puts full trust upon the Other Power, one will be born in the True Recompensed Land.[9] Amida made the Vow solely from his compassion for us who are wholly bound up with lusts and who have no way to escape from birth and death no matter what virtue we may perform. To have us the sinful become Buddhas is the very purport of the Vow. Therefore, the sinful who put full trust upon the Other Power are the right ones who will get born in the Pure Land. Hence: Even the virtuous get born in the Pure Land. Why not, all the more, those of us who are sinful?

"The moment we put our faith in the fact that we attain Rebirth (*ojo*) in the Pure Land by the

[9] See Chapter IV, Note 6.

Unthinkable Saving Power of Amida's Vow and the moment a wish to utter the *Nembutsu* arises in us, that moment we are taken in the arms of Amida, who will never forsake us from his embrace. The Original Vow of Amida makes no choice as to whether we are old or young, good or evil, the only thing important for us being *faith*. The reason thereof is that the Vow is for the deliverance of all beings who are heavily burdened with sin and fiercely burdened with lust. Therefore, once we have faith in the Original Vow, no other virtues are required of us, for there are no virtues that can surpass the *Nembutsu*; no fear need we entertain as to our sinfulness, for there are no sins that can obstruct the way of Amida's Original Vow.

"The *Nembutsu* is neither practice, nor virtue to one who practices it. It is no practice because the practice does not originate in one's self-will (*hakarai*); it is no virtue, because it is not an act of goodness originating in one's self-will. Since it arises solely from the Other Power (*tariki*) and is beyond one's self-power (*jiriki*), it is no practice and no virtue to one who practices it.

". . . I, Shinran, have no disciples to call as mine own. The reason is: I may well call one my own, if by my own self-will I can make him utter the *Nembutsu*. The *Nembutsu*, however, rises to one's lips solely by Amida's urge. If I am to call one who has thus come to utter the *Nembutsu* my own disciple, no act can be more arrogant than this. . . .

"Although I utter the *Nembutsu*, overflowing joy is hard to arise. No longing hastens me to the Pure Land. How might I accept this? To this his word was: I, Shinran, too had this doubt with me. Now I find you, Yuienbo, too have the same doubt with you. But be assured. In as much as no joy wells up in you for the matter at which you ought really to be overjoyed, your

Rebirth in the Pure Land is so much surer. It is the lusts that hinder our hearts from feeling joy. But all this Amida Buddha was well aware of beforehand. Therefore he called us 'lust-ridden mortals.' It was for the sake of the beings such as we are that the Other Power's Compassionate Vow was vowed. As I take things in this light, I am all the more filled with sweet hope. . . .

". . . Once faith is established in us, the work of our being born in the Pure Land is left entirely to the Will of Amida, and so no room is left for our self-will to take part in the work. The more we are conscious of our sinfulness, all the more we rely upon the Vow's Power. Then the meek and serene heart will issue from *naturalness*. As regards our Rebirth, we should in all ways and things abandon sagacious contrivance, and being enamored, heart and soul, of Amida, should constantly remember his Unfathomable Grace. Then the *Nembutsu* will rise of itself to our lips. This is *naturalness* (*jinen*). Where there is no self-will, there is naturalness. Naturalness is nothing but the Other Power. . . ."

To sum up, the *Nembutsu* is not merely to utter Amida's Name and to recollect his Great Compassion. It is the losing of our self-will in the Will of Amida. It is coming to our existential limits and *jumping over* the abyss which opens up before us. The door which was thought impossible to pass through now yields to a knock, and our limitations having been transcended, we find ourselves kings of the vast unknown. All the fetters of life which hedged us in on all sides fall away. Every possible piece of dirt and contamination attached to the human heart are shaken off. It is nothing else than the *Nembutsu* that bridges over the bottomless abyss of our sinful existence and *transfers back* our hearts into the Original Heart in the Pure Land. But here is the one thing we must not forget. The heart thus born in the Pure Land never rests in that country, for the heart thus purified is not the human heart. The heart, as soon as it reaches the Pure Land, comes back to this land of defilement and feels every human sin and suffering as its own. Thus, the heart, pure and repenting *in one*, blissful and suffering at *once*, is constantly reaching the other shore and returning to this shore—and this constant *transference over there* (*oso-eko*) and *back here* (*genso-eko*) in one act is the spiritual life or *naturalness*, the working of the Great Compassionate Heart.

V

Naturalness in Everyday Work

1

Those who have attained true spirituality have never talked in mournful accents of the sorrowfulness of life or of the bondage of karma, for they have learnt to transcend it. Not that the bondage has ceased to exist for them, but that the bondage has become to them as the form of freedom incarnate. Indeed that they have got their being in the unbroken chain of causation is true beyond doubt, but that is an *outer* truth. The *inner* truth is: From the Eternal Love do all beings have their birth. The spiritually-awakened man delights in accepting the bondage, and does not seek to evade it. He allows the *law of causality* (*inga*), moral as well as physical, to take its course, that is, he submits himself to it, he does not *sever* himself from it, he does not make any distinction between it and himself; he *identifies* himself with it, he becomes it, he *is* it. What distinguishes him most conspicuously from the ordinary man is his absolute passivity, his absolute submission to the law of cause-effect. What he has learned from his life is not that there is pain in this world, but that it is possible for him to transcend it into joy. This enables him to transcend the bondage. He simply goes along his way nonchalantly and fearlessly with the undying faith in his *inmost self* who is immortal, who is not afraid of death or sufferings, and who looks upon pain as only the other side of joy. He is thus in one way quite passive, but in another way altogether active because he is master of himself.

As this mastership is derived from a source beyond himself—from the Other Power, he is given full authority to use it as he wills; in truth there is no limit to his powers. Having lost the self-will in the Will of Amida, the Great Compassionate One, and leading the spiritual life in the bosom of Amida, he has life more abundantly than anyone else, with no self-seeking, no attachment; being equal to all circumstances, he is master of every situation. For it is Amida Buddha, and not his narrow self, that is operative here. Here is his *active passivity* or *passive activity.*

The ordinary man, on the contrary, has the law of causation separated from him. He thinks that there is an *external* agent known as karma or causation, and that this visits him according as he is good or bad. He does not realize that he himself is the moral agent as well as the law, that the law is inherent in his action, that he is the law-maker himself. To *separate*, to *divide*, to *discriminate*, to make a distinction is the work of the *intellect* or *understanding*, and where intellection prevails there is always the *dualism* of self and others. Indeed it is this dualism that weaves the net of karma and catches us unawares. As long as we are on the plane of the intellect or the self-centered mind, we cannot help groaning under the heavy weight of karma-hindrance.

The only and the most essential difference between the spiritual man and the ordinary man is that the former has that all-pervasive, selfsame, spiritual consciousness (*Prajna*)—*pure feeling*—which is *beyond* thinking, which transcends any form of distinction (*shabetsu*) or discrimination (*funbetsu*), while the latter has not yet attained the spirit's self-awakening. Living on the plane of the spiritual consciousness, however, does not mean abandoning or fleeing from the so-called worldly life. The spiritual life is not a *separate* existence of its own intellectual plane. The spirit does not ignore or negate the intellect; what it does is to *transcend* it, in the sense that it has its own government within the intellectual boundaries; and as long as it keeps this in good order, it knows no *outside* bounds imposed upon it. True spirituality is calmly balanced in strength, in the correlation or rather in the *identity* of the within and the without. It is in the world of relativity and duality, and at the same time is above it. The spiritual world is *at once* of duality and of unity, of distinction and of non-distinction, and for this reason karma is no-karma (*akarma*) as well as karma itself.

As for ourselves, it is only when we no longer separate ourselves from, but identify ourselves with the bonds of karma that we fully gain the joy of freedom. And how? As does the string that is bound to the harp. When the harp is truly strung, when there is not the slightest laxity in the strength of the bond, then only does music result; and the string transcending itself in its melody finds at every chord its true freedom. It is because it is bound by such hard and fast rules on one side that it can find this range of freedom in music on the other. While the string was not true, it was indeed merely bound; but a loosening of its bondage into the nothingness of inaction would not have been the way to freedom. The true striving in our daily life consists not in the neglect of action but in the effort to attune it closer and closer to the Eternal Harmony. That is to say, the self is to dedicate itself to the Universal Spirit through all its activities. This dedication is the song of humanity, in this is its freedom. Joy reigns when all work becomes the path to the union with Amida; when our self offering grows more and more intense. Then there is freedom. Then there is *naturalness* in our everyday work. We become no more troubled with karma, for we identify ourselves with it. We never fall into causality, because we are already it. Indeed suffering is no doubt suffering, but we have absorbed it in our spiritual consciousness where all such things as take place on the plane of sense and understanding find their proper meaning in harmony with the eternal scheme of the Universe. Joy expresses itself through the law of causality. The saving beam of Amida's smile of compassion is seen shining through the night of gloom. The world with all its sufferings, shortcomings, and dualities, becomes *one* with the spiritual world. Then in this world comes the Pure Land of Amida. This is the meaning of *Sukhavati-vyuha*—the embellishing (*vyuha*) of the Pure Land (*Sukhavati*).

2

The following incidents in the life of Shomatsu (1799-1871), popularly known as Shoma, will give us an example of naturalness in everyday work. Shoma was one of the great devotees of *Shinshu*. He was a poor laborer working for others, and lived in Sanuki in the island of Shikoku. His anecdotes are recorded in a little book, the *Shoma-arinomamano-ki* (*Shoma As He Was*). The following are taken from it.[1]

When Shoma was returning home to Shikoku from Kyoto, he had to cross an arm of the sea. While in the sailing boat with his companions, a storm arose, and so fierce was the sea that it seemed the boat would sink. The others lost their all-important faith in the *Nembutsu* and invoked the aid of Kompira, the god of the sea. But Shoma slept on until his friends woke him up. And, asked how he could sleep so soundly in the face of such calamity, Shoma queried back rubbing his eyes, "Are we still in this world?" We can say that he was

[1] The translations are taken from Dr. D. T. Suzuki's *The Essence of Buddhism*.

not aware of his being in which world, this world of suffering, or that world of perfect bliss—the Pure Land.
He was in all probability living in his own world of the
spirit. Life and death were like floating clouds in the
sky. They were not at all a matter of much concern for
him.

Shoma once visited a Buddhist temple in the
countryside, and as soon as he entered the main hall
where Amida was enshrined, he proceeded to stretch
himself out before the shrine and made himself com-
fortable. Asked by an astonished friend why he was so
lacking in respect for Amida, he said. "I am back in my
parent's home, and you who make this kind of remark
must be only a step-child." This is an attitude of mind
which reminds us of a child sound asleep in its mother's breast. He was so happy in the embrace of the
Great Compassionate One that the world of social for-
malities vanished altogether out of his mind. "Truly, I

say to you, unless you turn and become like children, you will never enter the kingdom of heaven."

Amida's Boundless Love for us and our absolute confidence in his Love are often compared to the relations between mother and child and have been specified by Gido (1805-1881; sometimes called Iriki-in), a *Shinshu* scholar as follows:[2]

1. As the child makes no judgments, just so should the followers of *Tariki* (Other Power) be free from thoughts of self-assertion.

2. As the child knows nothing of impurities, so should the *Tariki* followers never have an eye to evil thoughts and evil deeds.

[2] The translation is taken from Dr. D. T. Suzuki's *A Miscellany on the Shin Teaching of Buddhism*.

3. As the child knows nothing of purity, so should the *Tariki* followers be unconscious of any good thoughts they may cherish.

4. As the child has no desire to court its mother's special favor by giving her offerings, so should the *Tariki* devotees be free from the idea of being rewarded for something they give.

5. As the child does not go after any other person than its own mother, so should the *Tariki* devotees not run after other Buddhas or *Bodhisattvas* than Amida himself.

6. As the child ever longs for its mother, so should the *Tariki* followers think of just one Buddha, the Buddha of Infinite Light.

7. As the child ever cherishes the memory of its own mother, so should the *Tariki* followers cherish the thought of the One Buddha, Amida.

8. As the child cries after its mother, so should the *Tariki* followers invoke the Name of Amida.

9. As the child, thinking of its mother as the only person whom it could absolutely rely on, wishes to be embraced by her on all occasions, so should the *Tariki* followers have no thought but to be embraced by Amida alone even when in peril.

10. They should have no fears, no doubts, as to the Infinite Love of Amida, the One Buddha, whose Vow is not to forsake any beings in his embrace. When once embraced in his Light, no one need entertain the idea of being deserted by him.

Though somewhat repetitious, the above sums up what the *Shinshu* Faith is, and why it is called "Other Power Faith." Our "self," mortal, finite, imperfect, karma-bound, sinful, and bound for hell, can *live* only in the losing of itself in the Other (Amida).

On another occasion, when he had been working in the rice-field and was tired, Shoma came home to rest. When he felt a cool refreshing breeze, he thought of his Amida-image in the home-shrine. Thereupon he took it out and set it beside him, saying, "You too will enjoy the breeze." This may seem an abnormal act, but in the world of *pure feeling* everything that needs one's care has life, just as a child makes a living being out of a doll. In the world of *pure feeling* there is no consciousness of a process of personification. It is only the intellect which makes the distinction between animate and inanimate, sentient and non-sentient. From the spiritual point of view, all is alive and is the object of affectionate regard. Nor is this a case of symbolism, but a taking of actualities *as they are*. This is the life of naturalness.

When Shoma was ill while traveling, his friends carried him home in a palanquin and told him, "Now that you are back in your home, be at ease and grateful for Amida's Compassion." Shoma said, "Thank you, but wherever I may be lying sick, the Pure Land is always just next to my room."

3

From these we can say that Shoma's world was not the same with that of the ordinary people. He did not see things around him in the same light as they do. His eyes were fixed on a world beyond this, though not in the sense of a separate world. To the mind of Shoma, the Pure Land was not somewhere beyond this world, but right here. His life in this world was life in the Pure Land, where the sea is always calm and boats are steady. In the midst of turmoil, therefore, he had no cause to be afraid of anything. When he was sleepy he slept; when he wanted to sit up, he sat up; when the boat was tossed up and down, he too was tossed up and down; for he identified himself with the turmoil, and accepted whatever came as though unconcerned with consequences. Even amid the rising waves he felt the loving arms of Amida, the Great Compassionate One, and he slept in the boat even as he laid himself down before the image of Amida in the country temple. He was so happy in the embrace of the Great Compassionate One that he was *natural* in his every action, never being disturbed by any circumstances.

4

In truth, where is the further shore of no karma? Is it somewhere else than where we are? Is it to take rest from all our work, to be relieved from all the responsibilities of life? No, in the very heart of our activities, now at this very moment, we are reaching our end. In our own work is our joy, and in that joy does the Joy of our joy abide. Of our own work is Amida the fount and the inspiration, and at the end thereof is He, and therefore all our activity is pervaded by peace and good and joy.

In truth, O Thou Ocean of Joy, this shore and the other shore are one and the same in Thee. When I call this my own, the other lies estranged; and my heart incessantly cries out for the other. There will be no end of its sufferings so long as it is not able to call this home Thine. When this home of mine is made Thine, that very moment is it taken across, even while its old walls of karma enclose it. Everything remains the same, only it is taken across. Where can I meet thee unless in this my home made Thine. Where can I join Thee unless in this my work transformed into Thy work? If I leave my home, I shall not reach Thy home; if I cease my work, I can never join Thee in Thy work. For Thou dwellest in me and I in Thee. Thou without me or I without Thee are nothing.

Therefore, in the midst of our home and our work, the *Nembutsu* rises: "*Namu Amida Butsu!*" For here rolls the Sea of Love, and even here lies the other shore waiting to be reached—yes, here is the Eternal Present, not distant, not anywhere else.

Biographical Note

KENRYO KANAMATSU was born in Kyoto in 1915 and took his B.A. in Philosophy at Otani University. Following study under a Fulbright scholarship at Cornell and the University of Chicago, he received his doctorate and was a Professor at Otani University. In addition to *Naturalness*, Dr. Kanamatsu translated the works of Plato into Japanese and wrote a book on Plato's Theology and Cosmology which has not been translated into English. He was a lifelong devotee of Shin Buddhism. Dr. Kanamatsu died in 1986.

Biographical Note

REV. TETSUO UNNO studied at U.C. Berkeley, Ryukoku University (Kyoto), Tokyo University, and UCLA. He served as Minister at Buddhist Churches of America's Seattle and Senshin (L.A.) Buddhist Churches. He has taught in the Department of Religious Studies at California State University, Northridge, and Long Beach and in addition, at the Institute of Buddhist Studies in Berkeley, California.

Titles in the Spiritual Classics Series by World Wisdom

The Buddha Eye: An Anthology of the Kyoto School and Its Contemporaries, edited by Frederick Franck, 2004

A Christian Woman's Secret: A Modern-Day Journey to God, by Lilian Staveley, 2009

The Essential Charles Eastman (Ohiyesa): Light on the Indian World, edited by Michael Oren Fitzgerald, 2006

Gospel of the Redman, compiled by Ernest Thompson Seton and Julia M. Seton, 2005

Introduction to Sufi Doctrine, by Titus Burckhardt, 2008

Lamp of Non-Dual Knowledge & Cream of Liberation: Two Jewels of Indian Wisdom, by Sri Swami Karapatra and Swami Tandavaraya, translated by Swami Sri Ramanananda Saraswathi, 2003

Music of the Sky: An Anthology of Spiritual Poetry, edited by Patrick Laude and Barry McDonald, 2004

The Mystics of Islam, by Reynold A. Nicholson, 2002

The Path of Muhammad: A Book on Islamic Morals and Ethics by Imam Birgivi, interpreted by Shaykh Tosun Bayrak, 2005

Pray Without Ceasing: The Way of the Invocation in World Religions, edited by Patrick Laude, 2006

The Quiet Way: A Christian Path to Inner Peace, by Gerhard Tersteegen, translated by Emily Chisholm, 2008

Tripura Rahasya: The Secret of the Supreme Goddess, translated by Swami Sri Ramanananda Saraswathi, 2002

The Way and the Mountain: Tibet, Buddhism, and Tradition, by Marco Pallis, 2008